what
i
wish
my
teacher
knew

michelle muller

&

the 2017-18 ENG 10 students
of northeast high school

kansas city public schools
kansas city, missouri

KANSAS CITY – 2017

Copyright © 2017 by Michelle L. Muller

All rights reserved. This book or any portion thereof may not be reproduced or used in any manner whatsoever without the express written permission of the publisher except as permitted by U.S. copyright law.

For permissions & ordering information, contact mrsmuller.kcps@gmail.com
Reference ID: 21572091

For my students-
I hear you.

Contents

Preface 7

Morning Duty 9

1st Hour 17

2nd Hour 31

3rd Hour 47

4th Hour 65

(Planning Period)

6th Hour 93

7th Hour 117

Acknowledgements 135

Preface

I have wanted to be a teacher for as long as I can remember. My dad built a toy box in my bedroom when I was three years old, and the front of it had sliding doors that also happened to be chalkboards. He was one of my first students. He sat quietly, lined up neatly with all of my stuffed animals, facing those little, red chalkboards. He listened intently as I carefully taught them my entire preschool curriculum, and he patiently waited whenever I had to pause my lesson to discipline Quimby or John-John or Beans, my beloved monkey, bear and baby doll, who would inevitably start whispering and giggling every time I turned my back to demonstrate how to write letters on the chalkboard. My dad graduated from my classes around the time my little sister was old enough to start attending in his stead. By then, I had moved into elementary school, and I ended up accidentally teaching her how to read before she ever entered kindergarten. Unfortunately, Quimby, John-John, and Beans suffered from their young teacher's lack of classroom management skills and never fully embraced their academic potential.

I believe two of the primary reasons I was put on this earth are to nurture and to teach. I get to live this out at home with my own two children, but I also feel like there is a calling on my life to do this professionally, which is why I chose to pursue a formal degree in education before I ever graduated from high school. I love transforming the inaccessible into the accessible. I see the limitless potential in people, and I live to encourage and build up and call into reality those things which seem like adventures too big to undertake. I thrive in environments where I get to interact with people and where I get to pour my life into something bigger than myself. I love the proverbial "lightbulb" moments that I get to witness every day in the classroom as students make brand new connections that never existed before.

Life can be a terribly dark, difficult, lonely place, but I believe children can access hope in the classroom. I believe a single teacher can change the trajectory of a child's entire life through patience and determination and truth and grace and selfless, tough love. I don't believe there is a single child who is too far gone to be reached, and I believe it is my calling to take hold of as many as possible, and pull them into the light with me. Education literally opens up entire worlds to children. Education creates humans who are strong enough to hope and dream and question and create and wonder and thrive in the face of absolute despair. Education teaches children that they are infinitely more capable than they ever give themselves credit for, and that great things are possible if they are willing to persevere and work hard.

I want to be part of a world that honors the next generation for their potential and ambition. I want to live in a place that doesn't feel threatened by considering new ideas and taking risks. I want the people in my community to value character and integrity and diversity. I want my life to mean something. And I haven't yet been able to come up with a better way to make any of that happen than to roll up my sleeves and start impacting one life at a time through my interactions with the future generations found in the public school classroom. So I'm here, and I'm ready. May it ever be so.

m.m.

-Morning Duty-

This book really shouldn't exist for so many reasons.

At the time of writing, our distict is still seeking full accreditation status from the state of Missouri. As of October 1, 2017, the website for Kansas City Public Schools reports that only 9% of the students enrolled are White, with 91% identifying as Black, Hispanic or Other. 100% of the students in my school district qualify for free meals. The graduation rate is 65%. We serve a significant immigrant population, with at least 20% of the students not being native English speakers and over 50 languages being represented in our district.

I would say the high school I work in is a fair representation of these statistics. We currently have approximately 800 students enrolled in grades 9-12, with a teaching staff of 50. The four-story building was built in 1914 and was once the pride and joy of our city, with its grand entryway and opulent marble staircase. A lot has changed since then.

We are located in the Historic Northeast neighborhood of Kansas City, Missouri, which is home to a hugely international community, and is locally known to be an area associated with crime, prostitution, homelessness, drugs and poverty. This is a hard place to raise a family. This is a hard place to grow up. Nevertheless, it is an area I have developed a deep passion for.

My weekdays typically begin with an unwelcome alarm on my phone waking me at 5:00 AM, and just an hour later, I am finishing up my morning commute, driving down Independence Avenue and getting ready to turn onto Van Brunt. I usually spend my drive time savoring the dark quiet of the car, knowing that all too soon, it will be replaced by the noisy chaos of a crowded classroom. I mentally review the day's lessons, and often, make a few minor tweaks based on how I'm feeling or how my students have been acting lately.

That morning in particular was no different. I had been bothered for several days by my students' waning engagement in the lessons I was teaching. I was struggling to gain momentum, and felt that if something didn't change quickly, I was going to lose some of them for the rest of the year. I was desperate to connect, and to be honest, I was fed up with feeling like my lessons were irrelevant. So I walked into the building with my arms full, and my heart heavy.

As soon as I entered my classroom, I remembered that it was my turn to serve the dreaded "Morning Duty." If you are unfamiliar with this term, go ask a teacher, and you are guaranteed to receive either an eye roll or a groan. Or maybe both. My morning duty consists of joining three of my peers to monitor students in the school's auditorium as they trickle in through security between when the school opens and when the first bell rings. It's easy enough, but like all teachers, my to-do list is always about twenty items too long, and sacrificing precious alone time in my classroom once a week can be painful. Especially when I've already walked in feeling restless and discontent.

Regardless, I pasted on a smile and spent my time greeting students one by one, and taking a minute to catch up with the ones I recognized from my classes. For some reason though, with every brief student interaction, I had a nagging question in the back of my mind: "What aren't you saying?" I was just cranky enough that the politically-correct pleasantries weren't enough for me that morning. Their eyes belied their smiles, and I could sense a deep longing to be truly heard and known.

So, in those few fleeting moments, I called an audible and threw the lesson plan out the window. I have the luxury of doing this from time to time because I'm an English teacher, and we are sometimes known for being quirky. I decided to provide them with just one question as a writing prompt, and then monitor their time on-task for thirty minutes. I justified the new plan by using it as a way to practice extended, timed writing, which is a skill my students will need in order to be successful on their end-of-course exam, as well as any future advanced placement or college entrance exams.

But really, I just wanted to create a space for us to sit down together, to look each other in the eye, and for me to tell them, "I see you. You, personally. I see you, and I hear you, and you matter. And you are infinitely more valuable and capable than you ever give yourself credit for."

Based on their reactions when I presented the assignment, this lesson was as much a surprise to my students as it was to me. It quickly became obvious that some of them were much more comfortable expressing their thoughts and feelings in writing than others. Some of them dove in eagerly, while others balked at the notion of being expected to write for a full thirty minutes. Several in each class took ten minutes or more to get started, but for the most part, once they put pencil to paper (or hands to keyboard in most cases), the words began to flow in a way that caught us all off-guard. Students who had literally never engaged in any classwork to that point ended up writing multiple pages. Students who complained at the beginning of the lesson didn't want to stop writing when the time was up.

While I could tell that some felt safer than others in the assignment, the overall volume of work they ended up producing was stunning. As I sat for hours reading and responding to each one of them, my heart broke over and over again. Tears flowed, but their words were so precious to me. I felt as if they had fearfully, hesitantly handed me these tender little pieces of their souls, and I had no idea what I had ever done to deserve so much of their trust. I can tell you, though, it changed me. I am more patient now. I am more careful with my words. I have a much deeper respect for and admiration of them. And oh, how I love them.

It changed them, too. I have several students who were absent more than they were present, but since this specific assignment, they have missed very few, if any, days in my class. I have students who never spoke a word to me before, now giving me daily hugs. I have students who used to sleep through every class that are now attempting to engage with the content in a way that is creative and active.

You see, we can't undo what happened that day in class. They can't erase what they wrote and pretend it never happened. We now share a common history and connection. Like it or not, they are now known. Some of the walls came down that day. I felt like I had been standing at the door knocking all year, and they finally heard me. Some threw it wide open, while others only opened it just a crack. But we're in this together now.

As time passed, I found myself retelling their stories over and over to family and friends. I was so inspired by their courage and their passion, and I wanted the world around me to get to celebrate these things, too. And gradually, I began to consider the notion of putting their work together so that the people who care the most about me, and these kids, can also bear witness to their humor, strength, intellect, intelligence, creativity, passion, wisdom, and grace.

As I approached the task of compiling all of their writings into a single manuscript, I chose to edit their original work as little as possible. I wanted to retain as much of the voice and experience of my students as I could, while still protecting their dignity and privacy. To that end, I chose only to redact personally identifiable information to maintain the anonymity of my students. Beyone that, I simply formatted all of their writing to the same font style and size to improve coherence throughout the completed manuscript.

It is my deepest hope that I have honored my students through this work. May this serve as a memorial to this season of our lives, and to the depth of character they have had to develop just to survive. May their words serve to inspire and educate and advocate. And may we all never forget to slow down long enough to truly see and hear each other. How else will we ever make this work?

~

Sometimes school is tough, and days are long. It would make it a lot easier if my teacher understood what was going on.

I wish my teacher knew...

-First Hour-

Yea right school is really tough and hard because of what teacher teach, but the hardest things is that when teacher teach something that u don't really understand or understood. I really wish that all my teacher say or teach something that i don't know. I hope that they knew it before i say to them. Because some teacher is not the same like other teacher. All they know is to just teach they don't even care if you understand it or not all they know is to just teach and finished their jobs. I really wish that all my teachers teach all the student in the easy way to understand and learn more faster.

I hope that all the teacher understand how all the student feels or does not understand what they teach. One last thing i wanted to say is that all teacher teach all the student in the easy way so they all could understand it better. I really wish that they will help all the student what she or he struggle with.

~

That it's just school and football practice everyday and it's hard just to wake up cause i'm so sore from practice and it almost everyday. Sometimes it's just school in general like some classes just give me stress cause i don't understand what we are doing and i just get lost in the activity. Most times it's that i'm never really focused on school like i'm suppose to be and i need to fix that.

~

Today i'm going to write about something happy like the vacation i took this summer. The only reason why i'm writing about a vacation is because i really don't have anything to say about school being tough and that the days are long and i really don't go through anything rough. So now about my summer vacation. I went to texas what part of texas houston. We stayed for like a week and the weekend. Now about my siblings. I have four siblings two girls and two boys i have an older brother that is 26 and a little brother that is 11. I have an older sister that is 16 and a little sister that is 5. So for this vacation unfortunately it was only me, my sister and my mom. The only reason my dad and other siblings didn't go is because my mom dorve it was like a road trip so my younger siblings weren't going to be comfortable they were probably going to be complaining about everything. So my dad thought it would be best if my younger siblings stood home with him. My younger brother agreed with my dad so it was fine. So we left around 12:00 in the morning and our way to texas we talked about a lot of stuff and had fun. Me and my older sister were trying to keep my mom from going to sleep. Now we arrived to houston and omg it was so pretty but very hot. So we have family down there that i have never meet but did talk on the phone with so when we arrived i didn't know what to expect. They were very nice we arrived and they welcomed us with open arms and hugs. I had so much fun and i hung out with my cousins and a couple of there friends it was a great experience. We had something to do every day but also i did miss my younger siblings and dad and on the way back i was excited to see my borther, sister and dad but i was kind of sad since i had so much fun i didn't want to leave. Recently my mom told me that we were going back in december and i'm so excited i can't wait and my mom said that this time we were going to take my little sister with us. So i think it's going to be fun for my little sister because she loves dogs and they have the cutest two little puppys. I mean we have dogs out there big and to rough for my sister to play with.

~

I'm ranked 12 in the nation top 100. I graduate high school in 2 years. Cops pull me over they don't want nothing, they just want to lock up because they know i got a lot of bucks, but i'm bailing right out i ain't broke. When i was 14 me and my boys was riding thru the city, we pull up to the gas station while i'm pumping the gas tank 7 police cars pull up. I get in the car and my bro drives off. The police was chasing us we hit fast quick turns and we lost them but then a undercover cop seen us. Boom we hit a left, right, then we got on the highway. We was in nkc for a little bit then we got pulled over by a state trooper. My friend Jordan was a good basketball player i even think he had it to the league but he messed his career off he got possession's for them sales. This summer my friends and I played for the same AAU team the G-Code Warriors we were one of the best teams in the kansas city area. We played in a lot of tournaments we won most of them. We mostly play in kansas or in night hoops.

~

Not all students learn at the same pace. If we don't want to be bother we are going through something don't push us to talk in front of the class. Don't expect us to be perfect all the time cause at the end of the day we are still young and learning. When we do get off task don't start saying how our parents raised us or how we treat them. When teaching something i wish that they will go a little slower and when we ask questions don't say were you not listening it's not that we just need more help with it. They should be more sentitvie than what they are. Also, when we say we need to go to the nurse and you make us wait it shouldn't be like that cause some of us have medical problems. Wish should have a little fun once in awhile in the classroom cause we are always working.

Yelling at the students isn't gonna help slove the problem you're just gonna upset the student even more. I understand you want to teach and be all serious but you don't have to be serious all the time. Sometimes we need to take a break on doing our work so don't get mad right away.

~

My passion for basketball, as a term said "Ballislife" well this term is very accurate, and it's not just basketball' it could be any other sports that are out there but for me it's basketball. sometimes i use basketball to forget things you know when i'm in such a melancholy feeling, and gladly it always works. To me is very complicated because well, see i don't want to make it anywhere in basketball like (NBA , College team or whatever)

~

Why i miss so many school days and what i go through as a student. Studying is very hard for a student my reason why is because as a young teenager you're going through so many things and you plan a lot of things also because you also want to have fun as a teenager that's how i see it in my point of view. Some teenagers my age might have to go to work and they might have to work long hours as well for there family not to struggle. Also some students are drivers as well, just like me , so during the day i have to do lots of aarons for my older siblings and also my mother.

~

My life at home is very rough. My mom has lung cancer and she is all that I have been worrying about lately. I know that school is important and all but I think that these little moments that I get to spend with my mom are more important. I won't lose my focus in school even though she is going through this rough patch in her life. Everything that I do at home, work, and school is for my mom and to make her proud. I don't always get to see her or talk to her, but when she calls or texts me I answer no matter the situation. The situation is tough and I don't know exactly how to cope with it but I figured that turning to the church and staying focused and on task will bring better days. I know that all things happen for a reason. It's either a blessing or a lesson.
Music has really been helping me cope through a lot of stuff lately. If I'm not listening to music I can't focus. I mean, I can work without music but it kinda just helps me stay on task and not lose focus or get distracted. I like music as

you can see. I sing in the church choir every 4th Sunday, and whenever else I can. When I sing and listen to music it makes me feel like I don't have any of the problems that I know I have. Music is like my escape from what is happening in reality. I don't like explaining it like that because it makes me sound depressed but I'm not. I am very comfortable and content with my life right about now even through all of the problems going on in my life.

I also don't think many of my teachers know that I am bipolar and I have PTSD. I don't try to show these things around people because I learned how to control it, but I still have my days as does any other person. I am not currently on Meds as I should be but I have been working on ways to control my emotions in ways that an everyday regular person may see as normal. I don't know how to explain it, but I believe that I am different from other people. I really can't handle being in a huge crowd of people, I get very nervous and that's when my PTSD starts to kick in. Even with my mental illnesses I still find ways to cope and be happy with myself and all of my problems. It took me a while to understand that I can control it on my own and now I think I found the key to my happiness. I had to learn how to focus on myself and help myself instead of worrying what other people have to say and do. I think from here on out I will do good with whatever I want to do, if I stay focused on school, work, and myself.

~

I wish that my teacher knew I have trouble keeping control of my diabetes. It is a daily struggle and something that I am trying to get better at but sometimes it's hard when you don't know anybody else with diabetes around you. I wish that my teacher knew how hard it is for me to be happy with my work because I have OCD and I never feel like I can live up to my highest potential. I wish my teacher knew that sometimes I feel like the world is the worst place in the world because of the mean things people say to others. I wish my teacher knew that music is one of the one things that keep me sane. I wish my teacher knew that when I read it's almost like being taken to a new world, where everything seems so real and lets your imagination run free. I wish that my teacher knew that she's helping me because she is challenging me with some of these assignments and it's making me really think. I wish my teacher knew I have always been seen as the nerd in school but I'm happy being a nerd cause I have found friends that accept me just as I am. I wish my teacher knew I focus my best in the morning. I wish my teacher knew one of my biggest hobbies is cooking and I love to try new recipes. I wish my teacher knew that I want to major in business when i graduate from highschool and I wanted to attend KU.

I wish my teacher knew I used to have relaxed hair but I cut it all off and became natural because I wanted not only my hair to be healthy but my body also. I wish my teacher knew I am determined to make my parents proud and be the first one to graduate from high school with a scholarship.

~

Sometimes When I come to class cause I be sleepy and very tired and the days be long because of some of my other classes . Some It gets stressful but I can handle it , Things I like to do after school is play outside and have fun!!! with my friends and sometimes when I'm done with my homework I play videos games and watch tv . Other Things I enjoy is going to work so I can get paid , And I like coming to school so I can get my education and hang with my friends when the time is right and I want to keep my grades up so I will be successful later in life . Things I'm interested in is cars I like Bmw's and the Acura's TL because they are good cars and they last for a very long time .

~

People don't like to learn because they would get bored and tired that they want to sleep, and how to make things fun like word games using vocabulary or writing games, or even kahoot games. I wish my teacher knew that people like to get off topic for one to two minutes and then get back on time and how to make writing fun. I wish my teacher knew why I sometimes don't turn in my assignments and that I like video gaming, also that I love enchiladas and pizza. I wish my teacher knew that I kind of don't like english class and that I don't like writing either, also that I get off focus and just daydream about random stuff which makes me look focus and participating in the curriculum. I wish my teacher knew all computer shortcuts that are cool even on google docs. I wish my teacher knew I'm tired of writing essays because i have to write an essay in every class. I wish my teacher knew that I love technology and how it works and I like to code and mess with the codes. I wish my teacher knew that I want to read binary codes instead of english because it involves math to figure out the letter or number. I wish my teacher knew how to tell if someone is lying. I wish my teacher knew that I love being quiet and that she should have a quite game in her class and give the winning person candy. I wish my teacher knew that people are so sleepy in the morning.

~

I wish my teacher knew that I have car that I fix my car with my friends they all helped me to fix my car and I'm trying to improve my grades in all my classes so that I can have good job so I cannot lose my job and I will graduate high school after graduation I will go to work and get some money to pay off the bills.

~

I wish my teacher knew that i'm such a klutz i make stupid mistake without realizing it was a big deal. I always turn my work in late if it's not work that can be completed in class or dont get to turn them in at all. The thing about me and work is i never check my work at home unless on bored on a saturday. I dont mind doing work but there's got to be some thing to motivate me something like a giftcard or game card one of the only thing i would put work into is when there's something about game involved like any person if there's no reward there's no work.

~

It would make it a lot easier if my teacher understood what was going on,like waking up early, kids being loud,not understanding the work. Sometimes i wish my teacher would understand how i feel about school but i know that i have to finish in order if i want to finish school, and get a good job. Classes go by so slow slow the weeks be long, sometimes i understand the work sheets sometimes i don't . i don't get enough of sleep , i also wish teachers will understand that the school lunch is nasty, sometimes i wish i didn't have to go over work that i had already did before. I wish my teacher know that i try to understand certain work and i still get an F. i think teachers shouldn't make the whole class suffer when other students do something wrong, sometimes i think teachers should give us easier work when we come back for a break, also i think we should be able to listen to music without teachers thinking we're using our phone to text i think we should be able to use our phone when we had finish our work. But i also like how teacher's help me when i need help or give me an extra day to turn in work , i actually think teachers don't try to make the work hard up on us they trying to get us ready for what's next and what we need to know , and if i they need to work on certain things that we need to know , i know teachers want what's best for us deep down but when you having a rough day you don't want to do anything but teachers still have that day's as well but they still come to school for us and help us don;t gain an attitude nor not help us with the work , teachers help us for a reason they don't have to be here because of the money teachers come to work everything to help us learn when they didn't have to i know at times i can get smart here in their but i know how to treat someone with respect cause you earn respect to recieve it .

~

how much i hate this school . and my favorite team is the san francisco 49ers they were one of the first teams i new about and minnesota vikings. Favorite player is harrison smith

~

that i love playing videogames with my friends. The game that i like the most it's gta 5 i love playing online with them. When you play online you can talk to your friends and team up with them and play with other people that you don't know.

~

I wish my teacher knew how tired I am. I wish they knew how tired I am after the day and how I'm tired of working all the time. I wish they would slow down instead of rushing us. I wish they would give us less work. How I wish we had more time in lunch so we could get rid of stress and enjoy talking to our friends. I wish my teacher knew how hard it is to wake up early in the morning. I wish school started it litte late. I wish my teacher knew that I am thankful for what they are teaching us student I am thankful that they are sharing there knowledge with us. I wish my teacher knew that test are the reason our grade are going down. I wish they knew how sleepy I am in class because I get bored of them talking alot. I wish they knew my favorite sport is soccer and I play for the school team. How I wish they knew all I want to do is pass all the classes. I wish my teacher knew that all I want are A's. I wish they knew all I want to do is graduate and go off to college

I wish my teacher knew that I'm trying my best to do all the work - even tho sometime I slack off but at the end of the day I will get it done somehow. I wish my teacher knew I've been trying so hard to keep my grade up to A's but somehow I knew it wasn't enough.

Mrs. Muller
9/28/17

Sometimes school is tough, and days are long. It would make it a lot easier if my teacher understood what was going on.

I wish my teacher knew...

I wish my teacher knew that sometimes that someday's thing's can get a little bit over whelming and a little bit stressful. With someday's thing's can get a little bit piled up and how we gotta maintain everything and keep stuff together and workable for us and not only for us but for teacher as well. I wish my teacher knew how that some day's that it is okay for a teacher that it is okay for him/her to get involved with thing's and to make something's fun and exicted and espically sometimes and mostly on monday because thats mostly when people are still tired and out of energy.

-Second Hour-

that i'm trying my best to finish all my work in her class but i get distracted very easily, start to wonder off to space like i start thinking of so many scenarios which most likely won't come true; the other day i was thinking of what if aliens came to earth and started blasting at us would we have the firepower to go up against them or would we just surrender. Also what if the NSA were watching us through the laptop cameras here at school, like would they be able to see everything we do and can they hear everything we say it's stuff like this that get through the day just wandering off to space i know i should try hard to focus on my work but it's every hard when you have a big imagination.

Okay i'm switching topics now i lost interest in the first topic.

When it comes to school i feel like teachers are getting too nice, not that it's a bad thing but whenever you're too nice the student will treat you anyway they want and when you tell them what to do they'll take you as a joke trust me i'm saying this from first hand experience through this school year so far i've seen students get away with things they really shouldn't have but they do because the teacher doesn't want to write them up i think it's because they don't want the students to think wrong of them but sometimes i feel like you have to be mean to show the students you're serious about your job.

One of my teachers is really nice he/she has a mellow vibe to him but it sucks when the students won't let him/her teach they start cursing and get up start walking around the room at those moments it's fair to give the students warning but to let it continue all day now that's something else students should be written up for their actions to show them that behavior is not acceptable here at school; i understand they're with their friends and all because i was like that last year and i failed due to my actions, now this year i want to do right and move on.

I see the timer is almost up so i'll use this final minute to say this was actually pretty fun we should do this more often.

~

That i get distracted easily. And i work at a certain pace and it's hard for me to work in a loud class i like working by myself because when i work with others they are either not paying attention and it distracting. And i have to been shown what to do meaning i'm a visual learner. And you have to talk to me at a certain pass otherwise i will stare out of space and all the things you say will go in one ear and out the other ear. And i won't know what to do and i won't do my work. It's hard for me to remember things. Other people may learn different from me that's why i don't understand why i'm in a class with people that don't learn the same way as me. You have to speak loud in a voice that i can hear you because i have a hearing problem which makes it hard to listen to everything a teacher is telling me i may not hear them and just not care, may be something very important and i'm just like yeah yeah i hear you knowing i don't understand what is going on. And i'm very shy when it comes to me having to talk in front of the class like presentation and stuff especially if i don't have friends in that class. I'll stutter a lot and i'll speak low my heart starts to beat fast and i feel like i have to throw up. Other than that it's okay that's just my most difficulties in class.

~

I wish my teacher knew that I often feel sick and don't want to do my work because of it. I want to be able to focus and do the best i can but it's kinda hard when i have seasonal allergies during fall. For the most part i'm able to do the work but other times i just want to sleep or go home. It's a good thing that the work is pretty easy to me, otherwise i would probably be failing. I also wish my teacher knew how often i can't sleep.
I often fall asleep but then wake up after 10 minutes. It's annoying and causes me to not be able to sleep very well. That can affect the way i feel about doing work. I want to be able to do my work with all of my effort put into it but it's hard when i'm also trying to focus on staying awake.
I hope that when fall is over and my seasonal allergies are gone i can have a chance of enjoying school. I might as well try enjoying it seeing that i have 3 more years of it left. There are things i enjoy right now like weight training and math but i want to be able to enjoy all of it. I want to be able to go to class without feeling sick and be able to finish my work early so i can have a little time left to do what i want, or get the grades that i want because i don't have to worry about tiredness or feeling sick.
It's hard for me to get up in the morning and feel motivated to go to school, especially when i see my grades and there not that good. I've already missed like 15 days now which is not good,especially since we've only been in school for a little over a month. Now i'm just trying to bring my grade up from what it was and i'm doing pretty good at that but the next objective for me is to come every day. I don't want to miss any more days cause i want to be able to go to class and understand what is going on and be able to participate. It sucks to be one of

the only ones not being able to understand what is going on in class because i was too lazy to come to school.

~

That everyday school is the biggest stress for me. I get up everyday with the mindset of me getting my work completed on time. I worry about failing in class everyday. I worry about a whole lot, and it's really hard trying to make up my full 9th grade credits to become a full 10th grader. It's really stressful trying to make my parents proud and set an example for my younger siblings. I have to show them that anything is possible and to never give up. I was held back from my 7th grade year and had to repeat it over. So many times I wanted to give up but I didn't I pushed myself harder. The next year I was able to attend high school anything is possible you just have to show it and work for it. I will graduate in 2020 and people may doubt me but I'll never give up on school no matter how hard it gets. I have dreams in becoming a Pediatrician and working with babies. I can't live that dream if I give up and drop out, and that's why I'm still in school. I want a career not a job, I'm trying to become something in life I'm not working hard for nothing. School is really my main focus and I try so hard and sometimes I don't even be knowing how I be failing. School is really stressful and will really have you in a depression stage trying to rush all these things on your brain. Here I am a Sophomore taking some freshmen classes making up all the time I spent out of school. All I know is I will pass the 10th grade with all of my 9th & 10th grade credits. My dad always told me giving up isn't an option only losers give up and he ain't make a loser. So I'm trying to make him proud and take this W.

~

I wish my teacher knew that she's my favorite teacher because she never yells at me and never makes me stress over work. I want her to know that I try to do my best in her class. I try not to be late because the outcome of that would be 2 days of ISS. When I sleep in class, it's because I need help with the work, because nobody knows everything. She's the best English teacher i've had, but I got to do all of her work if I want to pass.

~

Something I wish my teacher new about is that I don't like when people look at me for a long time . It very weird and it sometimes freak me out. Another thing is that I don't like it when people ask really dumb question.

~

That I appreciate and am very proud of her because she always wants us to be successful in school as she always mentions in class and in our life in general. My teacher never gives up on us. Each and everyday, she keeps on being such an amazing teacher that we can depend on in class and handing out such informative works that we are able to understand clearly and get a good grade on.

I also wish my teacher knew that I am a very quiet girl who barely talks to anybody in school because I am timid, shy, and only focus on myself. Even though I am getting all of my work done in school and getting good grades in every class there is because of my quietness and not distracted by other people's talking, I get frustrated sometimes. Being timid means not being social enough, not going to make any friends in life, etc. I might always miss out on an opportunity of talking to someone who would have been a special person in my life in the future. I won't be able to help my parents translate stuff to English since they do not speak the language to people because I am timid and afraid of talking. My parents always think there is something wrong with me because I barely talk at all during school or anywhere and always want me to speak up more but they do not understand my feelings. Whenever a teacher assigns us to do a presentation in the front of the class or get into groups of people so that we can talk, I get very scared but they do not know it at all.

I may seem smart and I look like a girl who pays a lot of attention to work because I do not talk, but I actually am not. I struggle so much on assignments in classes especially algebra but I do not want to speak up to my teachers whenever I need help because again, I am shy for some odd reason. I need help even though I don't ask for it, as I am usually shy.

I wish my teacher knew how bad I want to make my parents proud who never went to college and dropped out of 5th grade (dad) and 9th grade (mom) because they were so poor when they lived in Vietnam and had to help their parents a lot of times in order to make money. I really can't wait for the day where I successfully graduate and I see the happy looks on their faces in the audience as I walk the stage with my graduation outfit, get my high school diploma, and exit the stage to the future that lays ahead of me. I really want to do great things after high school that would make them proud of me and I am waiting to hear them say, "I am so proud of you my beloved daughter."

I also want my teacher to know that I am scared of everyday. I am always afraid of what will happen next. Questions and thoughts fill my head because of this. What will happen? Will I die? Will someone I know get murdered? Will something terrible happen to my family? WIll something happen at school? Will I do something bad? I can never know the future that lays ahead of me. This is why I always hope to live my life to the fullest.

~

I wish my teacher knew that kids sleep in class because it boring. I also think we should do more fun activities sometimes. So we can relax are mind and not have to do work all the time.i Also think that waking up early in the morning gives some kid a headache.I also think teacher's and student's should be kind to each other.

I wish teachers knew some student's don't come to school because they want more breaks. I also wish the teacher knew i don't like coming to school sometimes.I say this because i don't like waking up early in the morning.I also say this because some teacher's give us some hard assignments and do not explain it really good.

My hope is one day i graduate from high school. I say this because once i'm done with high school i can focus on other thing's. Like working and helping my parents.Also i want to do thing's i never done once i graduate. I always wanted to travel the world may be one day i would have the chance to do so.

My favorite thing to eat is pizza and i like to drink milkshakes. My least favorite thing is lose i hate to lose when it is important.Something i hate about school sometimes is homework i can do it it's just when i get home i become lazy.My hobby is to play sports i try to play every sport the best i can. The two sport i like the best is playing basketball and soccer.

I also like to face new challenges in life. I like new challenges to help me gain new knowledge. Knowledge that can help me in the future that can help me face my problems.

~

I wish my teacher knew… that is hard to wake up 5:00-6:00 O'clock in the morning just to wake up for school and stay in school for 7 hours in school and i wish she also knew that school is stressful and tough sometimes because too much homework and it's so stressful when your grades and low and you want to get them up for basketball season or if i don't get my grades back up i won't play for the rest of my sophomore year and I don't want that to happen cause i really want to play this year too cause I love basketball i'll do anything for basketball that's why i want to get my grades up before Oct 13th so i can play this basketball season coming up. I wish all the teacher would know how bad i want to get my grades up right now i'm starting to go to school everyday just to get some work i missed out in all my classes and getting them done. I don't play when it comes to basketball i'm try my best just to get my grades up. I go in all my classes everyday just to ask them for more work and work just to get my grades up i beg them for more works cause mahn i am so ready for this season just like last year i was giving all them boys we played against buckets couldn't none of them guard me this year i'm comeback so hard nobody is going to stop me this year if i get my grades back up it"s over i'm giving anyone that comes my way on the court straight buckets after buckets after buckets i mean if i be in the gym giving 20 years old and up buckets imagine what i'll do to kids my age last summer our coach Coach Brown she put us in a grown man's tournament and we was giving them grown man's straight buckets after buckets after buckets they couldn't stop me or my team we was only 15 and 14 years old giving all those grown people buckets and we also got tournaments coming up this month on the 29th 30th and the 31st we about to go against other teams in Kansas our team is called the G-code Warriors last year league we won 20 times and lost 2 games that's crazy huh ? but mahn i love the team and the coach i have Coach Brown the best coach I ever had she will push you push and keep pushing you just to get you better if it wasn't for Coach Brown I wouldn't be playing how i play today she pushed me soo much and i got sooo good everywhere i hoop at everybody show me love and my games some love Coach brown used to make us run in the rain down and back from tree to tree she worked us out so much now all my teammates are good just because of all that hard work but Coach Brown was the best coach i ever had and i will always remember her if i ever go somewhere far with basketball i won't never forget about her I do this basketball stuff for her and my family I love basketball i've been playing basketball since i was 6-7 years old i stopped playing soccer because i found that basketball was my sport and basketball was for me everybody always used to ask me why you stop playing soccer i said it's not my sport anymore i like and love basketball now i just love basketball so much even words can't explain how much i love this sport mahn basketball got my heart me and basketball just attached to each other basketball always there for me when nobody there for me basketball the only thing that can really reliefs all the negative things in my mind basketball makes me forget about all the bad stuff that be going through in my mind and everything i'm dedicated to basketball i go to the gym everyday and work on my game people and my mom tell me take a break and i still don't i just keep keep keep playing cause this what i do mahn basketball my this my life basketball is over everything is what people don't understand first its God Family then Basketball.

~

That its hard coming to school after watching kids like babysitting kids andyour brother the time. Another thing i wish my teacher knew is that i have 1st floor 1st hour so it's hard for me to walk up to the 4th floor and be on time to class before the bell rings. The Third thing i wish my teacher knew is that some kids at this school has jobs after school and then they put their heads down in class their just tired of work and school . That why some children's attendance are bad because they have jobs or they have kids and started a life way too early.

I wish my teacher also knew that some kids don't comprehend as well as other students. It takes a while for other students to learn things. For example slow learners, they need extra time to learn or do the lesson instead of at home because their is no one to help them at home. So for kids that don't finish a lesson in the same day it's due then the teacher should send them to tutoring. I Also wish my teacher knew that some students struggle at home and have to do chores and have to wash clothes so sometimes they don't have the time of day to do their un finish work at home.

Another thing that i wish my teacher knew is that some children doesn't like to attend school because they feel like they are getting bullied or they don't feel smart enough for school because they have bad grades. Some kids don't come to school at all because they have bad grades and they feel like they can't get them up so they drop out. I also wish my teacher knew that some kids come to school just because their parents make them and they end up not caring , like coming to school because they want to see their friends.

The last Thing I Was my teacher knew is that some teacher give you a grade from your behavior and not the work you have done in class. I really wish my teacher knew that one of my teachers picks favoritism. The student was talking the whole entire class and got extra candy for nothing. It's always the same teacher and sometimes i want to change my class but the class is easy and i need the class to graduate. I also wish my teacher knew that her work is extra hard and its really hard for me to finish my work at home and in school no matter how many times she explains it. It just doesn't make sense.

~

I wish my teacher knew how her class makes school easy for me. Most of the work we do in class so when I get home it is easier because i don't have as much work to do. I be finished with my english assignments so I have more time to get all my other grades up. Also more time to play game and play basketball.

Also I wish my teacher knew how much school and sports is stressful. I gotta keep my grade above a C for each of my classes. It's always a certain deadline to have your assignments turned in. If the work not done in school you'll have to do it as homework. After practice it be hard to do work cause you be sore and tired.

In school it is easy to get distracted and I can't always stay focused. My friends might come in and try to distract me from doing my work. Sometimes I might come in made from something in the previous hour. If i'm mad i might just need a couple minutes to cool down then i'll be focused and ready to do my work. My phone can be a distraction sometimes I will get back to my work in after i do what i got on it for.

~

That i am now 17 just turned this tuesday. Not really non different bout it though. I remember wishing i was 17 when i was 16 because after 17 i would officially be considered an adult and i could do watever. But it's whatever now foreal. I'm still gonna b in school im still gonna be the same way. I just wish my life was better than what it is now. Im currently not working i wish i was cause making money is a struggle everyday is another day just wishing these days could pass by already and there's no more struggle with nothing. I wish life was easy and i could provide for anybody Especially family. I be feeling like im not shit sometimes when im just thinking bout my decisions, my life my future. Cus ik im better than that. Realshit my dad not even coo with me its been like 2 weeks we aint talk, i aint sad about it but im a little down cus thats now how it used to be. We used to b tight when i was young but now our relationship has just like faded away. He not happy with my life decisions. I aint gon lie ive messed up a couple times with his trust and iknow those are reasons for him to b upset but hes my dad ik they shouldnt give up on there son, and im his only son. If i ever had a son id try to be there for him whenever no matter what even if i dont approve of some of his decisions because young people make mistakes everybody do dont mean i shouldnt still b there for him. Like my dad got a problem with me Smoking Getting high cus he think its fucking up my life. Not even though Cause weed to fuck u up it just gets u high, i dont get how he got such a big problem with it if he drinks. He prefers me to do that then smoke cause suppose it dont fuck me up as much. But hes wrong, ig we both wrong Cus i be thinking to just stop doing both. But life be ups and downs alot sometimes i just need to chill not think about anything in it for a while at least try. Like kicking it with the homies not coming home till like sum in the morning on the weekend or friday sho sometimes i dont even come home and i get my parents get tired of it cus they just want the best for me. But i know myself i got this ima finish school im accomplish all my goals it just takes time like im barely still in highschool in 10th. They used to b young like me too ik they did the same type of shit my age thats why ion get why my dad such a trip sometimes he just boocie asf. Its someshit the type of relationship me and my pops got.

~

That its not easy living my life, and that's sometimes i get frustrated and feel so angry i want to kill. Sometimes i go through things and my head is full of criticism. That i no longer do the things i use to do cause i'm changed no longer feel things i was used to because i'm changed. I have no friends; i'm not into sports anymore, i feel like making money and having a job that's legal is kinda cool and feels goods. I like hanging out with my girlfriend and showing her a good time by treating her to outings and food, i really love her and hope god allows me to get married to her in the future; october twenty second makes it one year . I feel like people only respect you if you have money or you like to flex. I hate showoffs and people that seek attention, i dislike waking up at six o'clock everyday. I love your class the most i feel so relaxed and separated from nonsense and fools. Your an amazing teacher and you work hard for what you have. I like my favorite city year person from last year. She was cool i really miss her. I miss hanging out with my brothers but their into other things. Sometimes i feel like my big brother has mislead me years ago, so i try to stay afloat and make sure my little brother watches me do the right things. I love my mama she so sweet, a little cold hearted but i love her without her i would be here. The fact that she carried me for nine months is so touching, she could've said skip the pain and let me go. My dad, well i don't see him often but he's such a good dad i may not be able to talk to him as a man about sex or even other young adult things but he understands me as far as having a job and going to school. I go to church sometimes i remember when i went every sunday. I have this one guy at my church he stays giving me spiritual advice like let the lord take the wheel etc, i love him for being a brother of god, what a very inspirational man he is. Most importantly i love god he's opened so many windows for me and woke me up each and everyday he deserves the glory and praise for real. Without him there would be no you or me. I'm so thankful for him and his blessing. I'm scared of snakes and maggots literally my only fears. Im proud of the fact that im trying every single day. I'm good at making money. I want marriage advice i wanna know what it's like to really be with the person you love forever; it must feel good! I hate being angry it seems to takes forever to calm down. I wonder if the world has a time limit, if my time is coming soon. When i look at you ms. muller i sometimes think you're Ronda Rousey, she could honestly be you twin sister. My favorite quote/saying/verse is "I can do all things through christ who strengthens me." - philippians 4:13. I wanna be a computer programming in the future...

~

I wish my teacher knew that my mom can talk alot because i am tired with her talking but one day when i sit down and i realize that what all she is talking is for my future and i started putting it into my mind but but yet still it is very had for me and everyday she keep telling me one thing over and again and sometime i go mad because she keep saying one thing for the hold day and sometimes we come together and do thing in common but when you do one thing which is wrong you have put yourself in problem because that will be bad for you because the hold world will know about what you have done wrong but anytime i tell her what i want she will go all way to give what i want but she keep tell me not seal because her parent didn't learn her that and she keep presuring me to pray because my grandfather was a CATICIST and i was an ALTER BOY back home.And i love playing soccer because that is my favorite sport and i don't like to go to court because i alway think that when you go to the court the person that suse you need to spend and you also need to spend money so that why i alway stay out of problem and i don't like police.

I wish my teacher knew that I have so many problems going on. My life is devasted. School is the main thing I care about, but I stay messing up. Family situations are occuring at home. I come to school or public places trying to stay happy and even act like I have a normal life.

I wish my teacher knew that I'm trying so hard to be a good student. I've been struggling to come to school and stay in class. I've failed at being a daughter, student, girlfriend and a sister. I don't approve of the type of person I am. I want to be successful in life.

I wish my teacher knew that I want to be a veterinarian after I graduate from high school. I decided to go to Northwest university after I have enough money for my classes.

I want to make everybody in my family proud, including my boyfriend. I have the most supportive person at school who cares about me. I'm trying my best to be the better person I can possibly be.

    I wish my teacher knew that I like listening to R&b music. I like to sleep and play with my dogs. I admire to have supportive, caring teachers to motivate me on what's right for me. I hate the fact that people think or assume the worst on me. Sometimes about me.

I wish my teacher knew how boring I find school, that i'd rather be doing anything than be here. I wish she knew that I hate having to show up to school. That if I didn't have to show up I wouldn't. Also that I cant stay focused for long when im in school. Its hard to focus on something when you dont understand the assignment. I wish my teacher knew ive never written an essay because I dont know the format and all that stuff. I wish my teacher knew how tired I was and just let me sleep but I know that wont happen because im in school that why I despise being here. I struggle the most in English because the assignments are difficult/boring. If there was a way to make school fun then maybe I would actually participate. I feel like im not smart enough for school and thats why I struggle but I know deep down its just because I get lazy when it comes to completing assignments. During my time out of school I dont even think about it, I dont touch my laptop out of school because when you out of school I dont even want to think about it. I wish my teacher knew I dont like to ask

for help, from a student or teacher. I dont like to speak in front of the class. I dont like having attention on me because I'd rather be to myself.

-Third Hour-

I wish my teacher know that i suffer from cluster headaches which hurt a lot and i have them everyday. I wish my teacher knew that i really like to be challenged and sometimes finish very fast so sometimes my answers aren't on point on some days more than others. I wish my teacher knew that sometimes i don't want to come to school, only because i know that there is going to be drama as soon as i walk through the doors of the building. I wish my teacher know that i sometimes can be loud and i easily get off task when i'm around friends. I wish my teacher knew that i really don't get to spend my weekends the way i want because i work also, so when i come to school that monday, I might have an attitude. I wish my teacher knew that i'm not always on my phone for social media or to fool around. Sometimes there is family issues that happen and i need to check my phone often. I wish my teacher knew that i live in a house with my 2 brothers, 2 sisters, step mom, dad and niece so i get agitated very easy. I wish my teacher knew that i wish my teacher knew that i am a germaphobe so i really don't like when people touch me lol. I wish my teacher knew that sometimes. I wish my teacher knew that i don't like being bothered when i'm irritated, so if i lash out at them for trying to ask me whats wrong or anything else, its not personal or anything i just REALLY hate being bothered.. I wish my teacher knew that i also have a short temper so i can get mad easily so i might just be quiet =, so if i don't feel like answering anything its because im probably mad. I wish my teacher knew that my grandma has been very ill lately and i've been worried for her because she has been taking frequent visits to the hospital. I wish my teacher knew i'm a very social person so sometimes i can get off task. I wish my teacher knew that i have to work consistently for me to stay focused because the littlest things can throw me off.

When i'm not in school i like to play basketball with my brothers and my neighbors. We go to a community center in North KC and we spend about 2 hours up there playing against each other or playing against other people, My favorite food is pizza. I feel like no matter how much pizza i eat, i won't get tired of it like i do with other foods. My favorite color is turquoise. I really like green and blue, and i think those two colors together make a great color. My favorite movie series is divergent i like the action going on in that movie and i like the time and place it's set in. My favorite tv show is on CW and it's called The Flash. They have this whole section on CW called the 'Arrowverse" and it have a lot of Dc shows on there. When i get home from school i usually do chores, and go watch netflix. I'm currently watching season 3 of fuller house. I Just finished riverdale not too long ago. That show is good also. It's about a real life version of the comic book series archie and in season one they solved the murder of a boy named Jason. The next season is airing next month and They have to find out who shot archie's dad.

~

That sometimes it's hard for me to do my work because i get distracted easily and when i'm distracted i don't get my work done and i start talking and getting up and moving around and i can't control myself, And sometimes i don't understand what we have to do class and i don't do the assignment until i fully understand it when i like this class because it's pretty easy and you're a good teacher i like that you let us use earphones when we're doing certain tasks it keeps me from getting up and talking and not doing my work i don't like that my grade dropped from an A to a C just because i didn't do a certain task i also like this class because right after this class i have lunch and i get a 30 minute break from all my teachers when we do a assignment on one thing all the time i get bored of it and i don't like it because it bores me doing the same thing on the same topic like the 4th amendment like at first it was cool learning about how the law works and how the government doesn't follows the rules but after a while doing something over and over every day it becomes repetitive and i lose interest on it i also also hate writing essays i hate them with all my heart like i don't want to be writing 3-4 pages about something like i rather do a assignment with the class or a sheet of work because it's easier this one thing i don't like is that you don't let me in class when i'm late like ms.muller please let me in like you're doing too much like you're really going to make me go back downstairs and get a pass and mark me as tardy my favorite colors are blue and grey i used to play on team for soccer and i played as goalie i used to play football and baseball as well but i quit playing all them sports because i just stopped i like street racing i go watch races at night i also go out to the country and watch mud races there was this one time when i went to go see one and the truck almost flipped over it was crazy and they have really loud engines they have jet engines on them because they have a lot of power they also us jet fuel and the fuel goes for 10 dollars the gallon and it's lot's of money for you to fill up the tank i also like working i love working because it clears my mind like when i go to work from 4,5,6 in the morning and i bring my stereo and i'll be working all day with no problem and i'll be happy i just love being out in the country working no noise from where i live like hearing all the cops all the time going up and down my street it get's annoying

~

I wish my teacher knew my intentions, my goals, and my philosophy. I wish my teachers knew how I thought and the reasoning behind my decisions. An example of this could be why I miss so much school. I'm not a delinquent like most people who miss school. While my reasoning behind it may seem a little, whiny, or even ignorant, you could say. It still means something to me and it's my reality. My parents understand, which is why I'm allowed to do what I do. But anyways, the reason behind my absences is more than one problem, mostly a desire to pursue a career my school does nothing to help with. They say you come to school to learn and get your diploma so your chances of succeeding after high school is much higher, but I don't see it as that, at least in my scenario. I come to a school where most opportunities that other friends of mine, online and in real life, don't offer. It's very heartbreaking to find out you can't do something you wanted to do until later in your school "career," but at that point, you only have so much time to get situated with what you want to do. Me being me, I tend to take everything into account before making decisions, which usually takes some time, something I won't have taking the opportunities I wanted to take before after I was even offered. This is just one part of the problem, another problem I have is how I'm being taught. I'm not targeting any teachers whatsoever, because I understand they have a curriculum to follow and more than one class to teach a day, they can't just focus on one student. It's essentially the difficulty of the classes that bother me. I sit there bored in most of my classes. Not because I don't have things to do, not because I think I'm too smart to do anything, not because I refuse to do any work like a typical Northeast High School student. I sit there bored because of how fast I tend to get through things. While the class is sitting here doing repeats of work and concepts we've already introduced and practiced, I'm sitting there wondering off into space because I've already mastered the topic. Unless the work is time consuming in its nature, I fly through it like it's a second graders work, leaving me with nothing to do. Even homework could be put into the "time consuming" category, as it's only practice and typically does nothing to better your learning if you've already got a grasp of the concept. To add onto that, I'm surrounded by people that no one should be around. Screamers, talkers, and off-task students who are just a distraction. After years of having to deal with this though, I've learned how to focus despite the distractions around me. But it's still a very big annoyance to me and causes me to stray away from wanting to come to school. So I've talked about the annoying surroundings, the insane boredom I go through almost everyday, and the lack of opportunities I'm given in comparison to the average high school student. The last, and biggest reason I'll give is my productivity outside of school. While most people who don't attend school tend to slack off, do nothing but watch television, text their friends, and think of the day as a free day, I don't. I take this as an opportunity to pursue and learn what I want to learn, at a pace suitable for me. I'm aware that I won't always get what I want, with my classes being an extreme case of that, but I can always work towards what I want to accomplish despite the obstacles that I come across. I'm always working towards my long term goal, constantly putting in work in the background that might not seem evident to most, as the field of work I want to pursue won't even be related to school until I enter college. To give an idea as to how much I want to achieve my goals, I'm writing this paper on minimal to no sleep. This was caused by late night curiosity, studying, and practice. Which would explain my lack of structure, bad grammar, spelling errors, and lack of focus in this paper. This is not a very good representation of my writing but the point of the paper is to get a message across anyways. But as I was saying, I'm dedicated to achieving my long-term goals, doing whatever I have to do to achieve it. Now if you haven't understood how this relates to my absences, I'll explain clearly. Having goals unrelated to anything I'm doing in school, and learning things that I may need to know within minutes, I feel like staying home benefits me and my goals in the long run. I feel like the only thing that school is providing me currently is a blockage of practice/learning I could be doing at the moment, and my diploma. I come to school to be annoyed by my "peers," learn nothing or learn something very fast making the rest of the time boring, and what I see as a "waste of time" when I could be doing something else that would benefit me in the future. Not to say that school does nothing for my future because that is absolutely false, but for my personal situation, it doesn't do more than give me the go ahead to enter college. Not a single member of the school staff would find this to be a legitimate excuse for my absences, but I thought it was worth telling anyways so anyone who sees this won't get the wrong idea of me, hopefully. Given the time restraints, I'm not able to elaborate on the matter as much as I would like, but I somewhat believe this amount of information is sufficient enough for some to understand why I miss so much school. I only want to stay dedicated to my goals and don't want to be held back. So until I find something in school, or a school that I can pursue my endeavors and continue to get my education, I'll continue to miss school. After having done this for about four years, I won't just arbitrarily miss days, I try to only miss days that are far from quizzes or projects. You could even call it a "controlled" absence, as I try to take into account how long make up work will take, where we are as a class, the date until the next test or quiz, etc.

In conclusion, I just want to say that I love learning, I'm a very curious person. I love putting in work only to find that my hard work payed off. So I want anyone reading this to take into account who I am as a person; in theory, I should love coming to school, I should be very excited to come and learn something new, but that's just not the case. I only want people to understand my position and see what I see. Sadly, this paper isn't even enough to fully understand the situation, partly due to my vagueness. So I apologize for the lack of detail and hope the idea of the paper and reasoning was clear. If another opportunity arises in which I can explain everything fully, I'll be sure to put a lot effort into it so that any misunderstandings will be cleared up. I hope this doesn't come off as ignorant or anything along those lines.

~

that getting to class on time is harder than last year for me. I had a surgery and i can't be running to class like all the other kids. The surgery i had has been giving me problems from time to time but i try my best to get to class and do what i'm supposed to do. I wish they knew that i'm not as good at some subjects in school as i am with others. It's not easy coming to school and teachers expecting you to know every bit of work they give you. Most teachers are like that but not all of them my education is important. i've got people i wanna make proud so i keep pushing harder and harder every day as though it may not seem like i do because of how much school i miss. I have doctor appointments, sometimes i'll be extra tired, or i need to help do things around the house while my mom is recovering from her surgery

~

That i was going though a lot at home like my mom might be going to the hospital and i have to take 2 bus everyday just to get here. I love to do sports like i want to join the track team in the spring cause i love to run. I love to do and work on hair i st at home when i'm not doing nothing i go on youtube in like up hair tutors and i'll watch them in learn something new like i really want to try in go my own sew in in my hair but im scared i might mess it up. Another thing i really like to do is help kids i want to become a teacher, like after school i go to this church in help students with their work.in just help around the church. In the summer i like to go summering in hang out with my friends and everything but this summer didn't really do as plan because of money but (*name redacted*) in i go together a couple of times this summer in had fun. I like to make music on how i be feeling like if i'm upset r something i just start writing down stuff and make a song out of it i already made two songs one about love in one with my ex we sat down in write a love song together but its not finished. I like to listen to music tht tell the truth whenever i listen to a new song i listen to what the people is talking about one of the song i have on repeat is DO RI MI- blackbear it a good song i really like it.

~

I wish my teacher knew that i hate when we in class i be trying to learn and the rest of the class is acting silly and not paying attention to the lesson and it just irritate me, I wish my teacher knew that i "HATE" bullies , I wish my teacher knew that i am actually trying hard trying to pass all my classes , and that i don't sometimes understand my work so it's hard for me to do , and that i be having long days so sometimes i be tired and frustrated.

I wish my teacher knew that i don't like to talk when i'm angry , upset or irritated, i wish my teacher knew that i don't like waking up and coming to school all the time because i be tired , and that i hate walking up these stairs everyday because i be tired :(, i be out of breath , and i also wish my teacher knew that i really hate drama , i don't really be trying to be in it but things happens for reasons sometimes .

I wish my teacher knew that i have 12 siblings and i am adopted so it's actually sometimes hard for me at times but i try not to think of it very often so it doesn't upset me but the best thing about it is not i live with the best woman i could ever ask for , and i love her to death . most definitely the best mother ever to me and i love her for that . no one knows the bond we have , she's my bestfriend.

I wish my teacher knew that i'm not from kansas city mo and that i am from (*place redacted*) , i usually drive there when we go down to visit , that's where most of my family stay , i moved up here when i was 4 years old , so it's been a couple years since i've been moved up here , sometimes i be wishing i can move back because i sometimes hate it here , and i like to be with my family because they make me happy .

I wish my teacher knew that i had a dog's , one of my dogs ran away but not far , i caught him but this old lady was driving and my dog was crossing the street and she almost hit him until i stepped in the street and then she put her car in park and got out with her key and stabbed my dog and i almost fought her because he didn't do nothing wrong but tried to run back to me , also he's name was "jocko" and he was a little lucky animal , he looked like a little hot dog .

I wish that my teacher knew that i like to go shopping, and have fun with my friends, and go to the movies with them , and i like to get my nails and toes done , and get my hair done , and i like going swimming , and i like going skating , i like working because it'll give me something to do when i'm bored . so that's what all i wish my teacher knew.

~

School is not easy for me I don't think school is easy for anyone i personally enjoy school but, Then again i dont think its for me i get frustrated and irritated and if i can't do the work i won't try or i will try sometimes. I get frustrated because i know if i try that i'll get it done , and if i dont then ill just feel like a failure in life in any subject i get mad and frustrated. Cause either i wasn't there or didn't pay attention or was confused from the start of the project . Such as math i get frustrated and mad because the numbers and letters mix up and i can't do it i mean i can but i have to really focus . At home i don't focus because i have so many distraction and it's hard for me to get it done .Music helps me alot because i can clear my mind and music has songs for everything from being mad , sad , happy , frustrated, calm , or you just wanna jam. I also play sports so i have to have everything on point for volleyball, soccer and other sports BUT let me get to the point LIFE is not easy for sum of us Students some of the kids get made fun of and get picked and they don't have the same clothes as the rest of kids some students have a style of their own and unique while a lot of kids try and be the same and look the same and act the same . Some people don't like the music you play or listen to the will talk bad to you and be disrespectful and , Rude about it or make fun of you i don't get people and why they do the things they do god didn't put us on this earth to be the same and act and look alike he put us here to be different and to be our self . Some students think school is easy for them ive seen a girl do her math homwork in 10 minutes like some subjects are easy for some people social studies adn chemistry is my favorite like ik that of the top of my head .

~

I wish my teacher knew about all the problems i have to deal with at school and at home. Teachers really don't know anything about some students, we tend to hide and cover up our problems. I wish my teacher knew that i have problem with writing, i can not come up with ideas or anything. I Have trouble making my essays longer and not being able to fit more details into anything. I hate writing and typing , i never have any good ideas or any good stories to tell. I wish my teacher knew that i am afraid to ask for help because i don't want to seem like a dumbass. I lose my train of thought so fast i tend to forget what i'm doing. I honestly dislike writing but i do love reading. I enjoy reading so much, i imagine all the things happening in the book and it's fascinating. I rather read than to write about things i don't like writing about. If i were to write , i'd like to write about anything that makes me provide facts and proof about a certain object or thing. I love watching sports, i enjoy watching my favorite football team and love that winning streak that they have right now making the Chiefs top of the division for the mid west. I'm a big fan of sports mostly football and soccer. I love that i finally have a best friend to talk to about sports and watch games with him. I really love that feeling when i go support him at all his games win or lose as long as he continues to do what he loves doing , i'll always be behind him every step of his journey. Im Proud of my best friend.

~

I wish my teacher knew… That i like to play basketball only in the the gym because outside it makes me feel uncomfortable. I hate reading because usually when i'm reading a book the words are to small for me to see. I love writing because it brings out a good side in me. I like working in groups because i like communicating and working together as a team. I like school mostly because i get to see my friends everyday.

That when it comes to individually working i sometimes struggle. I hate when a teacher expects me to do something that he or she already knows i can't do. I hate when the school feads me crappy lunch. My favorite color is red. I don't have a favorite t.v. show because i like watching all shows just about. I want to go to college and play basketball and maybe go to the NBA.
My favorite hobby is to draw.

I've only been in 1 fight my entire life. I love cars, especially foreign ones.

~

I wish a teacher knew nothing so they could stop talking to me about B.S stuff . I did not eat breakfast. My favorite color is orange. I am sitting in a black and grey chair Ms Muller is talking now a girl got up out her seat and walked to the back to miss muller. Someone just sneezed and everyone is copying how she sneezes. Ms. muller is walking around the room checking people's work.

People in the room are talking out loud.Someone is playing music through headphones.I am humming right now.Someone just cused in the room.Someone is copyingIts words on the wall in Ms.Muller class.People are typing on their computers.MS.Muller told me to stop clapping my hands.Even though it was a great beat I might add. Ms.Muller is telling us to wrap it up because it is time to leave class.

~

That I prefer handwriting every assignment I do. I honestly don't like typing or using computers when working on projects, essays, etc. Working with computers are difficult at times but I know i'll eventually have to get comfortable working on them since i'm going to college because that's where all my work will have to be. Also I wish my teacher knew when I'm not in the mood, has an attitude or just upset I rather work alone & just sit by myself not talking to anyone to keep calm. I wish my teacher knew the way I explain myself or the way I talk may come off as being smart or having an attitude but I don't mean any harm I just like to get my point across because I'm a very argumentative person, also I understand work when it's being explained to me one on one or peers breaking it down to me, when taking notes over it, it might help out as well if i study them and take my time. Homework isn't a problem I just sometimes forget about doing the vocabulary so I wish there was another way to remember doing that.

~

How boring class can be sometimes. How many questions i have in my brain but i'm too scared to ask cuz i might be judge. I wish my teacher knew how bad mi past was and how bad mi days are going. I wish my teacher knew how many times i've been discriminated just for being hispanic. I wish my teacher knew how much i love singing and how fun it is. I wish my teacher knew how much i enjoy music and how much it helps me. I wish my teacher knew how many times i've been laughed at but i still stand. I wish my teacher knew that even tho i look like someone tough and someone who always happy i'm very soft and i have a soft heart. I wish my teacher knew how much i enjoy making people smile and make there day a better day. I wish my teacher knew how many times i've wished everyone could be happy and didn't had problems. I wish my teacher knew how difficult it is for me to know that most of mi family are in Puerto Rico.

I wish my teacher knew i'm not to much into sport i'm more into anime and gaming. I wish my teacher knew how many times i've cried cuz i dont have a dad and how many times i've cried bcuz i haven't been able to make someone happy. I wish my teacher knew that even tho i smile and make people smile i hide how i really feel. I wish my teacher knew how much i hate people talking about others. I wish the teacher knew how much i'm in love with my girlfriend. I wish my teacher knew how much i hate those guys who call themself a "MAN" just cuz they treat girls bad or the hurt them like mi opinion is there not man there coward and there someone who wasn't taught what's right or whats wrong. I wish my teacher knew how much it hurts that people don't like other people. I wish my teacher knew how many times i've tried to change and to be a better person but i can't. I wish my teacher knew how horrible it use to be for me in my old schools. I wish my teacher knew how much i despite those who think they kill just cuz they did "something" to them but they just hated them. I wish my teacher knew i annoying it is when people wont shut up in class. I wish my teacher knew i've had to experience earthquakes. I wish my teacher knew how much i hate that people don't have respect for teachers. I wish my teacher knew how boring class can be. I wish my teacher knew how much i like creating story but i'm too shy to show them or tell them. I wish my teacher knew i love french fries and nerd candy and gummy. I wish my teacher knew i don't know what to be when i grow. I wish my teacher knew i want to learn how to sing better. I wish my teacher knew how many people tell me to go to the voice ,america's got talent, etc. I wish my teacher knew how much i enjoy having fun playing games, reading, and spending time with my girlfriend. I wish my teacher knew how fun video games and anime are. I wish my teacher knew how i feel about class and how i feel about teachers. I wish my teacher knew i'm too shy to tell her she looks nice today. I wish my teacher knew how much i hate fake friends. I wish my teacher knew how nice i am and how nice i can be. I wish my teacher knew i love smiling but i can't so i have to fake it. I wish my teacher knew how much i like snow and how much i enjoy living because i live to see people i love smile. I wish my teacher knew i suffer in class.

I wish my teacher knew how many times i've been angry but i've smile to make others smile. I wish my teacher knew i love my friends and love to make them happy but i hate to see them suffer. I wish my teacher knew how many times i've suffer in silence but i still smile. I wish my teacher know i enjoy her class even tho i don't like english. I wish my teacher knew i love roleplaying (>W<). I wish my teacher knew how many times i've been stabbed in the back. I wish my teacher knew how much i enjoy typing but i'm too shy to show cuz i feel like they will judge me. I wish my teacher knew i sing when i'm alone more cuz i feel like people won't like my singing. I wish my teacher knew i love to see her smile and everyone's. I wish my teacher knew how much i love to mess around and make people feel better and not feel bad or sad. I wish my teacher knew i want everyone to be happy and have the bests of days. I wish my teacher know how difficult it is to keep a fake smile when im down. I wish my teacher know sometimes entering her class changes mi mood from down to happy. I wish my teacher knew it makes me feel more relief typing and expressing myself in words. I wish my teacher knew how mad i am with my cousin.

~

That I have a life after school that I try my best to do all my work, but sometime I can't always finish in time. That day my teacher failed me cause it wasn't done right. I wish my teacher knew that I have a nephew that i be watching almost 24/7 cause my sister is a drunk. And when I try to get time to do my work I get yelled out over things I haven't even done. But when I do have time I just go to 9th street it's a soccer field I go there to clear out my head from all the problem from my life. The soccer field is my space of freedom. Yes I should be doing my homework but I don't want to do my work there it feels like I'm in prison and 9th street is my freedom. So I try to do all my work at school so I won't have to do it at home and anything I haven't got done I do it during lunch or whenever I have all my work done. So then when I do go home I can just worry about nothing and it's less stressful. But times teacher get on my case about doing another teacher work in their class and it makes it harder for me to do my work when I'm denied to finish my work when I have nothing to do in that teacher's class I thought teacher are suppose to motivate us to do our work to push us along when we have their work done so we can finish up any other work so we can have a good grade. There's time I have hard days and I just in a bad mood cause I got into a fight with my family. And I just listen to music to give me good vibe and the teacher tells me to turn off my music or put up my earphones. They don't know I work 100% better with music than hearing the whole class just yelling and talking and it distract me from learning if I don't have my music to keep me on track all my classes I'm passing thank god but it's only the first quarter and I have three more quarters to finish so I don't know how the rest of this year will go for me. I wish my teacher knew that I have 4 different job and it's stressful I have to watch my nephew, do school work, work at my job, soccer practice, and soccer games it's stressful when I have to do so much and my teacher just think I'm 100% every time I'm in their classes. When I'm actually 17% but they won't know that because I feel like the teachers don't care how you feel only if you do your work so I just pretend I'm okay. And when I do that I'm struggling more on doing my work and like when I don't do my work it's like the teacher acts like I haven't done their work for a whole school year.

~

I love to dance I been Dancing since I was 3 My grandma Started me Putting Me on the table telling everybody get they money out I start dancing They start giving me money i had enough for my diapers food and everything I needed. Also I wish my teacher knew I Like to cook I watch my momma and Grandma Cook all the time then they ask me to help One Day i had to cook for them They really like it Soo i just be cooking it up in the kitchen

~

That math is my favorite subject even though my grades say otherwise, I like or use to like school up into middle school things started to change i started slacking more with each year that passed by. I got lazier and nothing really motivates me anymore i just want to graduate and get a highschool diploma doesnt mean much to alot of people except for me and my family id be the first to finish highschool but im not sure if im going to college yet hopefully id like to attend college but my grades arent doing that good i wont be able to get any scholarships for academics and i dont want burrow money and end up having to pay my student loans for 20 years later after i graduate and on my career im still not sure what i want my career to be yet but i have two options primary i want ot be a nurse but i have alternative routes if it doesnt go as planned cause i now their is going to be a few bumps in the road but we can detour around and still be able to get to our destination but my second option is becoming a mechanic its not a high paid job but im not looking for anything that would earn me millions of dollars it would be nice but id be happy with what if i earned as long its something i like and being stable, i like money who doesnt but im not greedy never will be i know money doesnt mean everything and its true it cant buy happiness but it can sure as fuck buy me a house for me and my parents do soemthing for them because they done so much for me . raising me money cant do that it can buy you things you want or need but it doesnt buy you manners nor teach you things you need to know. Theres a few things i started realizing about school which made me slack alot. I started thinking real deep about it like most of the things we learn wont really mean much in the "real world" like what is x going to do for you in real life unless you go to college to become a math teacher. There is somethings in school that you do need. But school doesn't really teach you how to do taxes or other important stuff that you need to know. I wouldnt exactly say im an angel but i am a good kid i respect people when people respect me regardless if its a stranger or not like you ms.muller i have respect for you and i would like to know if you are going to teach english 11 so i can try to switch to your class i like the way you teach you are one of the few teachers that i like having. But because im a good kid doesnt mean i do bad shit we all done it like you ms muller you proably went out done something you shouldnt like go to a party and drink or got drunk w freinds who knows that is your life ive done alot of bad shit also like go out and drink go out and spark up a few blunts but dont take this cursing in a bad way its just my way of showing you got my trust .

~

I wish my teacher knew that I have a short attention span ..

~

I wish my teacher knew that she didn't have to take her job so serious. She could do have job and still have fun, with us and herself. We could do fun, challenging, and easy thing. I also wish my teacher knew that we don't have to learn about history in english class. We should just be learning how to read and right. I wish my teacher knew that this accesignment is doing to much. Writing for 30mins is boring, very boring. I wish my teacher knew that school isn't as easy for us as they think it is. Waking up at 5-6 o'clock in the morning and wait for 5-10mins for a bus to come pick us up. I wish my teacher knew it's hard not getting on our phones.

~

I wish my teacher knew that essays are really annoying and that government surveillance starts getting very boring and I wish we worked on something different everyday. I also wish my teacher knew, that somedays we deserve a day to just get caught up on work, and I also wish she knew that I would like to do free writes a lot more in her class because they're better then talking about Government surveillance everyday. Government surveillance is a very boring subject to write on, even though we need to know about our rights but most days it is very boring. PRISM is also kinda the same thing because is also about government and still very annoying and boring. My goal is to achieve all my goals I have in life and become a nurse and have a family. I also want to have kids and raise them to be respectful and very caring to everyone they meet. I also hope to hope to make enough money to support my family and get a house and be able to pay all my bills. My goal is to also get all passing grades this year I don't care what grade it is I just want it to be passing.

I like basketball I love it I'm Kobe also I hate school it make me sleepy I love 2k and Madden My fav basketball player is Kobe bryant I hate going home it is boring I love to fight I sleep alot I listen to music My fav rapper 50 cent and nevin gates I hate country, rock, jazz all that bull Oh and Mozzy My fav rgil to I also think Black people are irritating and anoying and I'm gone smack the IT guy if my computer don't get fixed
Coach
[illegible]

I'm from the
I'm not gone front
I can't date white girls it's nothing wrong it's just that seem a lit wired to me like for feal They be like suck my toes and then we got to fight

-Fourth Hour-

I wish my teacher knew why I was so goofy and playful, because I use humor to mask my sadness and depression. I wish my teacher knew how much my parents don't understand me, they call me anti-social when the only people I don't talk to is them. Wish she knew how my mother thinks I hate her when on the other hand, I strongly feel like she doesn't give a damn about me. I wish she knew how my siblings get treated a lot better than me. Wish she know that honestly, I hate group work. I like to stay to myself. I wish she knew how music is my favorite thing in the world, how music keeps me sane each and every day. I wish she knew that i'm a visual learner, I like to see how things are done so I could do it myself, or reading. I wish she knew how much I hate being asked questions there's no chance I know the answer to, and how I hate being asked the same thing twice. I wish she knew that the main reason I had trouble staying awake is because at night I don't fall asleep until after midnight, even if I turn my phone off and lay there with my eyes closed, it'll take a couple hours or so to fall asleep. I wish she that I can never keep a pencil for more than three days, which is why I always need one of her's, I usually lose those too. I wish she knew how important my hair is to me, and my physical appearance in general. I wish she knew how fast and easily I catch feelings for people since I don't get too much at home. I wish she knew that all my goals are right now are making more money, since I basically upkeep myself (clothes, shoes, etc.). I wish she knew that I can't wait till my birthday so I can save for a car, a better phone, and better clothes/shoes. I wish she knew that even though i'm doing a lot better than most people I feel like i'm in the worst situation, I don't know why I feel like this, some might say i'm a bit self-centered and conceited, but even I tell myself I am. Lastly, I wish she knew that I love coming to school everyday because I try and get away from home for as much as possible.

~

I wish my teacher knew I was tired and that i like to sleep. I wish she knew that school doesn't have enough energy and hype for me. I wish my teacher knew that I go home and eat like a cow and that i don't sleep early or even go to bed on time i wish that she knew how to fly and could cast wizardly spells on us. I wish she knew that i want the world to be like the walking dead. I wish she knew my birthday. I also wish she knew that my favorite color was turquoise. I wish she knew that i'm competitive yet calm. I wish she knew i like to snack every few minutes. I wish she knew i enjoyed beauty and makeup. I wish she knew that I'm very imaginative. I wish she knew i had sisters and brothers. I wish she knew my mom. I wish she knew i imagine a tiny person on her dancing while she gives directions. I wish she knew that i am lazy and that i also love noodles and rice. I wish my teacher knew that i like finishing assignments early. I wish she knew I've been in an accident. I wish she knew that i have turtles and that i race them with my boyfriend (*name redacted*). I wish that she knew how to make me tiny so i could fit in my tiny race car or even run with my baby turtles. I wish she knew that i didn't like the apollo 11 assignment. I wish she knew how to busy rhymes. I wish she knew that i wanted to do the hamilton broadway play. I wish she knew the hamilton play. I wish she knew i like to draw. I wish she knew to let us write poems. I wish she knew it would be awesome if she taught by song. I wish she knew a lot about our us government. I wish she knew i wanna be a princess. I wish she knew that i want to be a scientist and cure cancer. I wish she knew that i also wanna be doctor. I wish she knew that this class makes me sleepy i wish she knew how gravely tired i'm getting right now. I wish she knew that it would be radical if we could go to school now i wish she knew how much hair is in her head. I wish she knew that i got less then 2 hour. I wish she knew that we don't like extra long assignments. I wish she knew that these kids are bad. I wish she knew how to sing to us. I wish she knew that i dont live with my dad i wish she knew i had a passion for makeup . i wish she knew that i am a good actor . in i wish she knew what my real name was. I wish she knew how to solve all our problems. I wish she knew that doing homework was hard for me. I wish she knew not to give us another assignment after this. I wish she knew her door was creepy. I wish she knew how to tell us spooky stories. I wish that she knew that i like her classroom. I wish she knew i liked writing but not when i have a topic.

~

I like jrotc,i enjoy being on special team last year and i am doing it again. Special team is like a sport team we go out and compete against others schools. There are 3 differnt teams you can try out for color gaurd they do the flag Armed they do the riffle and unarmed we do the drill. There are also some really good school and school that don't even try. We go against schools like lee smit you know the good rich school. We the only school in kcps that travel to drill meet.

That some of us have to work after school. We can not sit and do homework all day. I understand it mandatory but we get tons of homework from every class and it not easy. What if someone didn't have a place to sleep that night you give out the homework. And they have to jump from place to place trying to find a place to sleep and something to eat let alone homework. We should get more than one day per homework because we have to pace our time to get it all done and by the time you finish it another teacher throw more homework at you. How can we get the exercise we need if we are sitting at a table for hours. What if your wifi want off that day you have a lot of homework that do that day and you can't get it done.

~

I wouldnt recomend that you read this whole thing, there are a lot of things I wish my teacher knew. For instance I have ADHD, i take medicine for it even though I don't believe that I have it. This may be the reason I am never truly on task, however when I see something that i really want to do I put all of my energy and mind on it. This is why sometimes my writing is just a complete mess, i will just pour out everything that's in my head and go three hundred different directions with it. It is also why sometimes my writing is relatively creative. I have a lot of ideas in my head for different things. For instance right now I am working on a book called "I, the One Who Walks Away From Omelas.' it's a story based off a short plotless story about a city called Omelas (oh-mah-las.) Omelas is a city that seems to be perfect… Almost a utopia if you could call it that. The city never used slaves or gotten into war, and is pretty successful in the economy and society. However the city has one abomination, the reason the city has been held in peace for so long, a child, hidden beneath the city, desperately alone, locked alone in a small room and considered a nothing. The child is only fed cornmeal and water twice a week, deprived of everything the people have, its innocence taken along with the hope for ever getting out of the place. Everybody in the city knows, they just accept it, and those who don't tolerate it leave the city and don't return, for they cannot disrupt the city's peace for those who do accept it. Some don't believe in the kid and want proof, so they are taken to gawk at the child of Omelas and know the truth. My book is based on the escape of the child and the underlying truth to the harsh reality of the sacrifice of one for thousands.

  That is just a small explanation of the book, I kinda went a little deeper than I expected to but Oh well. Another thing I should inform the teacher on is that I am actually a ward of the state. I have been for three months, and next week I will be going to court to see if my parents are convicted and will sign over certain rights to us so our aunt can adopt us. The reason all of this has happened because during the summer I had a job and I returned home one evening and my sister and brother were both very bruised and told me they were beaten for going to get food from a store down the street, because our parents had not left anything to eat when they left and I was not able to get any for them, so they took some of the emergency money left for them and walked to the store, They found out and you can guess the rest, this wasn't just a one time thing, my mother's husband was never a pleasant person, he always was a bully and loved coming up with weird punishments for us, our whole lives, he dictated us and would starve us periodically, we would stand for hours on end for something as little as making a noise that was too loud. I was tired of it so we called our aunt and told her everything, she called hotlines and the police and we were placed in her care unofficially. Hopefully this next week it will turn permanent and official, she is one of the greatest people I know and I would want nothing more than to be like her when I am older. I hope the only time I have to see my mother or her husband again is in court. They are some of the most vindictive people I have ever met, and I am glad I don't live with them anymore. Now I know this woman is my mom, but she stood by and drank herself into a hole as her husband actually broke us and her, she would wake up with bruises she didn't know how she got, but we did, he wouldnt let us tell her. We were terrified of him obviously so we weren't saying anything. Many times over the years there would be so many dfs workers at my house, but they never did anything, they would come and look at us but we had no proof, our bruises were 'self inflicted' or not serious. I couldn't let my siblings live like that, it just wasn't something i could bear to rewatch asif a flashback for me, I had to get them out, so I contacted my aunt, and now I get to watch them grow up like normal kids, just normal, happy kids. It's too late for me to be completely normal, I am always going to have this underlying knowledge and hatred toward my mother and her husband, no matter what I do. So i throw myself completely into something and stick with that to focus on, such as Kpop. It is one of the few things I actually do truly find comfort in. Anyway Im done with my rant… sorry.

~

all the hard things I go through. For instance how busy my schedule is. Some days I don't even want to get out of bed,let alone got to school and to cheer practice. Every day there's a new assignment in every class. There's days when I wish I didn't have AP classes and I was just like everyone else. I be so tired, sometimes I go to sleep or I don't even attend class. Then after a "hard" day doing my work in class, here comes cheer. We learn new cheers and dances everyday that I can barely remember as it is. Football game every friday! Then homecoming is coming up and we have to perform, that's another thing on my list I have to take care of. My momma doesn't make it any better. Chores, chores, and more chores! She has me do so many things, it's ridiculous. It's like i'm the maid and I don't even get paid. She always have me watch my little sister like I don't have a life. Let me not start on our petty arguments though, I can go on for hours. I try my hardest to leave every weekend just so I don't have to deal with her 7 days a week, 5 is enough. Yet, she still has a problem with that too.. Friends? Yes I have those. It don't matter what i'm doing i'll always stop what i'm doing to make sure they're ok. Jungling all these are a hassle, especially trying to keep my grades aline. So far they're good, but I know eventually I'll fall off. I honestly just need a day or a month where I get to chill out with no responsibilities.

~

that I have trouble staying focus. I have a lot of distractions at home. Examples would be my siblings, tv, laziness, procrastination and so on. My siblings are the biggest distractions EVER. I have a little brother who loves to annoy my like it's something he has to do EVERYDAY. I get out of school at 2:20 but since I ride the school bus home I get home a little later. Somewhere around 2:40 or so. Once at home I have almost less than an hour to do my homework before my other siblings come home. The sibling that I'm talking about is in 6th grade. His school let's out at 3:10 but he also rides the school bus home so he also comes home a little later. He comes home around 3:24. I have 2:40 to 3:24 to be able to relax at home and start my homework without my siblings around. When I do start my homework I end up daydreaming. I just think about random things, and by doing that I end up wasting time. I always notice myself daydream and get back to my homework but sometimes I don't get the homework or I just suddenly get bored and I end up giving up. Even though before I get home I tell myself to start on my homework as soon as possible. I just seem to not focus even when I'm by myself or have no distractions. I don't understand why that happens. I get mad at myself for not being able to focus when I want to focus it's so frustrating. My mind is ready but my body won't cooperate. So I end up doing something else like laying around or maybe taking a nap. I get even more mad at myself when I hear my sibling running into the house, up to my room and start banging on my door. "*(name redacted)*!" And he starts making weird annoying noises. I try to ignore but he doesn't seem like leaving until I tell him to. I just wasted the perfect amount of time to finish my homework without distractions. I only get out of my room to eat dinner. When my little sister sees me she greets and ends up talking all about BTS. My sister and I are big fans of BTS and I can't help but listen and fangirl with her. You know when I end up doing my homework? I end up doing it at night when all my family members are going to sleep. That's when I do "focus" to finish my homework. That's not good at all. I should really manage my time. Focusing is really important to me because that's how I am able to get things done and understand. There is so many other distractions or obstacles that get me to focus. I have to do chores, help my siblings with homework, or watch tv. Sometimes I also have trouble focusing in class because the littlest thing can get me distracted. For example if someone starts drawing or doodling I'll end up watching them. Focusing is hard -well at least for me it is. But there's lots of time when I do focus and I'm proud.

~

During the past few weeks things have been very stressful, I've been having home issues that's dealing with me, and trying to balance out school is really hard. For one i can't settle for a b i know i have potential to keep all my grades and A so i try to work as hard as i can because when i see my grade card i want to be able to see complete A's, i really don't understand why a B makes me mad, i just feel like a failure at times. Well anyways i don't feel comfortable with telling all my business, i am very secretive i like to get better on my own, but sometimes it does feel good to get things off your chest . Well for starters trying to balance a friendship and relationship is very hard. My boyfriend doesn't like none of my friends at all, he always bring up how they are bad influence and things but we have two different perspectives. I love my friends and wouldn't trade them for the world, they have been very big impacts on my life and have grown so much on me during the past years. My boyfriend is very irritating at times, but just like my friends i wouldn't trade him for anything in the world neither, he have helped me become a better person, he helped me love myself for me and always stuck by my side through the rough times plus he knows how to deal with my bad attitudes. Well we got into a big argument about my friends, i know that in a relationship you have to sacrifice at times, so i started to kind of distance myself and not hang with them a lot. I was really sad because i felt like my boyfriend didn't understand that i can't do everything with him, he's not a girl. My friends bring out a different me i like hanging with them and gossiping you know what girls do. Now i feel like i'm losing one of my closest friend, which is really making me feel some type of way. I just wish at times god could talk to me and tell me the things i need to do right but for now i'll just let everything fall into place. Bad things don't last forever right ? Another thing is my attitude, i kind of have a short temper so i do seem to kind of get smart with grownups if i feel disrespected. I have been trying to work on it, but it's really hard when people test your patience. At times i try to stay by myself and just calm down, but then you have 50 million people telling you that you acting different it's not a win at all. Last year in the beginning of January i lost one of my close friend who was 13 going on 14. That was a hard pill to swallow, but i can't help that she crosses my mind every now and then. I'm pretty sure you know my pain to lose someone close to you, knowing that we will never speak again, hang out or do nothing. I can't face the fact that she's gone and never coming back. She died in very bad car accident which lead to her car falling off a bridge down in Texas. well anyways her, her cousin or Auntie didn't make it, only her mom made thank god. I try not to let things affect me as much but i'm the type of person to bottle my feelings up because i think no one cares about what i have to say. I never understood why we live to die…. I mean yea you should find something/somebody to live for but is it all going to matter in the end…? Sometimes i want to go far away to a peaceful island that no one knows about and find my inner self. I'm stuck between making the people around me happy that i'm not happy and no one ever ask am i ok or just to check up on me. I'm not saying everyone should do it every day but if we're close i need for them to understand that i'm going through things that i don't talk about to them, so a text here and there can really make my day. Well except my boyfriend. He's really amazing and i can't wait until the future to marry him!I really love everything about him like you just don't understand it's like at times i be looking for things that's right in my face. He always make sure i'm good, put me before himself, he done sacrificed so much things for me, and when he tells me he love's me i can actually believe him because not only does he says it his actions prove it.

~

I wish my teacher knew how stressing it is to finish homework and classwork. We have jobs well some of us, I have a job and I have chores at home to do also. Also when kids act up it disrupts the whole class like? Send them to a different school or something I'm trying to get my education. When I graduate I'm gonna go against everyone in this country class of 2020 for jobs and if my act score is low? Then what it's going to be hard to get into college. I also hope they knew if they're having a bad day not to take it out on us. We didn't do anything to them if you come rude to me guess what I'm gonna come ride back to you even though my mom raised me different. I also wish my teacher knew about how much things people go through at their homes. Not everyone is from a good wealth family. People are struggling they have to work in order to get food on their table. I thank god I work because I want to. But you guys only see our good parts at school just because we don't show it doesn't mean we don't go through anything. But you guys don't understand that. If you guys assigned homework and someone turns it in a few hours late you guys don't even try to give them half credit? They didn't ask for that life working all the time having no time for school they didn't ask for that they were given that life and just because you guys had a silver spoon in your mouth doesn't mean anything. And yes education comes first so if they turn it in later y'all should accept it? But no you guys wouldnt understand and I also which my teacher knew I have a life other than school. I can't be doing homework all day everyday. I got a life, other then school I also wish they knew that sometimes to stay out people's business like? What does it have to concern you i know that seems harsh but then again after you tell a teacher your business they might go report it or go tell other teachers then they feel bad for you like no just sometimes yall need to mind yall business. I also wish my teachers know that I'm barely waking up in the morning like you guys expect us to give answers our brain is barely waking up. Then also I wish yall would know to stop saying if you don't wanna do work then don't come to school to students because students will go to court with their parents for missing days so i think that is very irrelevant to say. OKAY now to things about me. My favorite color is purple, I'm fifteen years old, I got a part time job to make extra money just incase I need anything I don't like asking people for things not because of pride just because I know I can go out and make money and get it myself. I like to keep personal things to myself because I don't trust a lot of people. I'm actually a very nice person just sometimes I have my days we all do. I have 5 brothers and 2 sisters yes then including me which is 8 kids. I'm in the middle of them, if you're wondering if we fight um yes a lot but our bond is something no one can break. Idk if this matters but idk what to say anymore when i grow up i want to go to the marines and become a master gunnery sgt. After i want to become a homicide detective and i wanna pursue my dreams and not my sisters, friends nor my parents. I want to become something better then my parents. They always told me they want me to be better than they were. But since we're talking about my parents my mom is a RN and about to be a paramedic and my step dad he work somewhere in warehouses i forgot tbh. My daily routine when i get home is clean, do my homework and if i got time after then go walk my dogs at the park if not just walk them down the block then get ready for bed because my homework takes about 3-4 hours sometimes even longer. One cool fact ig about me is i can play 3 instruments violin guitar and piano. Thats me and my thoughts.

~

That sometimes the lesson are hard to understand so if you could break it down it would help because when we start to do our own work it really hard to know what i'm doing. I like this class since I only have 3 more classes to go. This class is probably the comfortable class in my hours. Cause the environment is friendly and people are nice and they don't get in your business. This class help in lots of ways because it english and i like reading. When we reald old stories it kinda hard to know what they are trying to say. I think the teaching is great. This class is like a sign that it almost noon so you know people get tired and they get lazy to do their work. It would be really nice if on friday we could do a short work and then have a free time. But I know its not gonna happen but thinking about it help. I know we have a lot of work to so because we're falling behind the other classes. So you can argue to that. I think this class is the shortest class because my other classes seem so long. But I think they have the same amount of minute. As I said before this class has a nice enviroment so I really won't complain too much. It just this class is all away at 4th floor and it takes along time to get here. So if the class was at the bottom it would be really nice. Imme you can't change anything about that but just sayin. I hope someday this class can go on a field trip it would be so fun. Maybe we could go to a museum or zoo but we probably won't have funds to pay for the trip. We could go to a place that has the famous authors spots and go around to seem others. Plus write about what we learn during our trip. I really hate the sound outside of the window they been doing fixing since forever. I thought they already finish but i guess i was wrong. This is my only AP class so i'm proud to be in here. Cause that makes my parent proud. At least now they have something that they could say positive about me. Instead of always blaming me. It about time for parent teacher conference but i don't think my mom would come. But that alright i could just show her my progress report. My mom use to come but she has to watch my brother now, so since last year she don't come anymore. I think she would come when i'm a senior. I just hope I don't repeat grade. This year i could've been in 11 grade but i fail fourth grade so it sucks. I hope to graduate this grade and class.

~

What i wish my teacher knew is how capable i am to do my work good. I wish she knew how much i like this class and not hate it i actually learn in this class compared from my other teachers. I have my days where i slack around like today. I wish she knew i like cars alot. I wish she knew that i knew i could achieve my goals alot better and that i barely let bad things affect my performance in your class. I wish she knew i wonder how her life has been working in her prison teaching class, was she terrified ? was she scared to go everyday knowing bad things could happen ? the risk she was taking and how it affected her emotions ? i wish she knew that i was raised excellent by my mom and that i messed it all up when i started hanging around people not associated with the same goals i have in life. I wish you knew how bad i used to be always getting calls home because my behavior in school. I used to do always do dumb things on purpose just to anoy my mom not knowing i was making her mad and sad. She always depended on me that i was a influence for my brother and sister that everything i did they did so she said to act good because everything bad i do thier going to think it's ok or good even tho its not. I wish she knew i used to be so dumb when i was little that those gift cards at the stores i'd always take them not knowing they had to be paid and i'd give them to people. I used to cause alot of trouble between my parents they'd spend days arguing over my issues.

~

I wish that my knew that I have a lot of stress that goes on in school and at home. I also want my teacher to realize that I try to turn in all of my assignments on time but sometimes when I try that in all of my classes I fall short of that goal. I know that you deleting the assignments might help me in the future such as college and even the jobs that i might have will have writing in them. I want you to know that I will try my very best to get the best grade that I could get and be on my best behavior. I want you to know overall that I won't make your time here at northeast hard like some other kids that might do that. Being at school is stressful but sometimes it is my escape from the stresses at home that are not necessarily on me but on my parents. Yes I do know that what my parents stress about is not my stress or supposed to be mine at least.I still feel horrible asking them for money or just anything at all knowing that there already stressing about it. School does create a lot of stress but it also can relieve some. Especially when there are teachers that understand what I'm going through and helps me get through whatever it is im stressing about. I also like the teachers such as yourself who prepare me for college and other life activities such as jobs. Such as when you put a time limit on the homework and no late work, that gets up ready for college because that is exactly how it is but instead of a paragraph or something small its projects and essays, many more. I usually try to stay to myself when it comes to school except for like two or more friends I'm not some popular girl to the whole school but I am becoming a very successful women and doing whatever i put my mind to so that is all i really care about at this moment in time in my life. I just want teachers who make school fun to be at because if teachers make it boring when they can make it fun then there isn't many that will even come to school if they had that choice. I on the other hand will never miss a day of school if i didn't have too even if school is boring or not because i'm not here to have fun im here to learn and get an education and do what my family never did or break the cycle i should say for my little siblings. I want my brother and sister to grow up with me as their role model that is one thing that i will so proud of doing. I want my brother and sister to have a different life then i did growing up so they to can be successful when they are my age. I just want you to know that you're doing an amazing job as a teacher do not try and change for anyone because you are helping me and all of your other students be successful now and in the future. I do not like the teachers who come to the class to try to fail their students because that is not helping them be successful that is just being cruel. I also do not like teachers who take what is going on in their life out on us, and students who do the same thing i feel like if someone has a personal problem leave it personal or just at home and not school. Oh one last thing that i like that you do is that you try to interact more with your students and try to get to know them better, which not a lot of teachers do so thank you for that. Because you never know what is going on in someone's life and they just need someone to talk to you can be that one person to help that other person. Especially in northeast there are a lot of kids who do not have people to lean on and teachers may not know but they could be that one person who saves someone from killing themselves or stop someone from being bullied without actually saying anything about it. Teachers have that effect on student if they just would pay a little bit more attention to their students. School is hard not only from school work but from other kids and teachers can make it easier if they just tried more and didn't give up on the students were not as bad as some teachers think.

~

That in some of my other classes I'm failing and I know that it can be my fault there is one class that I feel doesn't teach well which is chemistry she only decides to teach when administration and I really don't understand why I have an F if she doesn't even give us work to do. I get annoyed in that class also because we test every friday and I really don't understand anything in there I wish i could change classes because I know if I tell her this she won't listen to me because i'm a student and to be honest i don't want to get administration involved but i do care about my grades. One of my favorite classes is english because I have a teacher who teaches very well and at my speed and I feel very good about this class I just have to get it together and do the homework i get assigned cause when I go home I just forget about school. At home I have time to do my work but later at night like around 8 pm because i do have to do chores and sometimes when my mom has to do stuff i watch my little siblings which it's not a lot but sometimes when you're a teen you want to do stuff like go hangout with your friends but when you have responsibilities it's not really possible. I am not much of a morning person which is probably why I always say "I don't like school" but to be honest school is my future and I won't be successful if I don't do good in school and do my work so I can have that I want and especially because i want to make my parents very proud of me and in order to become a doctor like i told all of my family that. I have always struggled with math but the math teacher that I have I feel like we don't get along because everytime I ask her what do i do to bring my grade up if there is no work on google classroom but she always tells me " it is not time for that were taking notes right now" which is no help at all because i do not want to get in trouble by my parents for having a really low grade ! One thing that I like to do outside of school is to go out with my friends and my close cousins because everytime I ask my sister if she wants to hangout she tells me yes and all last minute she cancels on me and prefers she prefers her boyfriend over me which annoys me a lot because i had asked her to hang out before him but never again will I ask her because she dissed me for him. Now when she asks me if i want to hangout i always tell her i'm busy or that i'm already going with someone because to me it was not cool. I like to go out with my mom a lot because it is really fun to bond but lately things aren't the same between me and her, we bump heads a lot and argue which i think we just fix cause she is like a bestfriend to me. This year i got really close to some of my new friends that i barely talked to my freshman year but i did lose many of my old friends which sucks but life goes on and friends come and go. Not that long ago it was like 2 weeks ago I had my quince and I had so much fun it was so stressful planning it but it was so worth it and a quince is like a sweet 16 but kinda different and in my opinion better !! one of my favorite things are ice cream, going to worlds of fun, chinese food, trying different things and i also like doing the spicy noodle challenge. The last time i did the challenge i was with (*names redacted*) i was the third to finish honestly it was so hard to finish them and my mouth was on FIRE i ran downstairs to get the whole bag of ice but it was making it worser and there was no milk and only 2 popsicles we were fighting over the popsicles but i just put a hand full of ice in my mouth and let it sit there because it was burning. My dad took the whole family to worlds of fun because we have season passes and he hates roller coasters but we got him on the prowler and he hated it !! For me school is a little stressful because of all the work and my grades dropping but i just have to get it together and do all of it so i can bring my grades up i just need someone to help me out.

~

I wish my teachers knew that teenagers in 2017 have been said to have the same levels of anxiety and stress as mental institution patients in the 1950s. I wish my teachers knew that mental illnesses are valid, and should be a valid reason for late work or class absences. I wish my teacher knew that we have lives after school, and that adding on homework and extra work on top of our afterschool activities isn't the best idea. I wish my teachers knew that we have chores to do at home, some of us have to cook dinner and clean and babysit and do laundry and wash the dishes and sometimes that takes all night. I wish they knew that some of us only get 4-5 hours of sleep every night and that it's really hard to stay awake in the mornings. I wish they knew that depression and anxiety and ptsd and bpd are all very valid things and that we're not just teenagers trting to fit in. i wish they knew that not everyone is up to something. If we are late to class we might be at the counselors or the bathroom, and that we shouldn't be penalized very hard if the reasons that we're late are real reasons. I wish my teachers knew that if we're trying to express ourselves, they should let us. We should have time to be teenagers. I understand that you're getting us ready for college, but we should be able to hang out with our friends after school, and still be successful. I wish they knew that dyed hair, piercings, tattoos, makeup, and our clothing choices are our choices, and we shouldn't be taken any less serious than we would if we didn't have those things. i really want teachers to know that we are living, breathing humans that deserve the same amount of respect as someone our age. Some of us really need music to focus, and we're not just trying to ignore you. I wish they knew that not everyone is the same and we all shouldn't be assumed to be the same. We're going to cuss. I know it's disrespectful to you guys, but not everyone feels that way. We cuss to get excitement out, to just joke around with our friends, and to just feel different. We should be responsible for our behavior and actions, but i'm not sure if our actions should be held to an airtight standard. Some people don't have money to spare, so if we don't have a notebook or colored pencils or a poster board, it's not always the fact that we're tired/lazy or that we forgot. Cellphones will almost always be out. They're our window into the outside world. I know you guys always want our undivided attention, but sometimes we just really need a break. Not every student is going to be the easiest to handle, but please be patient with us. Some of us are going through a lot, and it'd be amazing if you just got through it with us. Its hard to always stay focused, so if someone is dozing off, or if they have their head down, just ask us if we need a drink or something, and get back to your lesson. I personally like to put my head down a lot, even if i'm not tired. Sometimes i just have a headache or i want to rest my eyes, but i'm still listening to everything you're saying. Please accept and appreciate us. It's hard to make and deal with changes and if we decide to shave our head or wear colored contacts or ask you to call us by a different name, just go with it. It might be a phase or it might not be. We are still trying to figure out who we are,and it would help tremendously if you guys supported us, because we don't always have the support at home. Some people have had to grow up much faster than others, so if we act grown and are stressed or working or really anything that might interfere with your lesson, please bare with us. If we have food in your class, please let us eat. None of us really try to make a mess, and i know if it were me i would at least try and clean it up. Some of us dont have time to eat at home or couldnt during lunch, so we just try and eat anywhere we can. Please don't judge or exclude any of us. We need support and reassurance and it would help a lot if we got that from you guys. Dont call us out or expose us in front of people. If we're missing assignments or we messed up a test or anything like that, we'd appreciate it if you'd pull us aside or told us privately after class or something like that. We try our best and it's honestly kind of heartbreaking when you announce in front of the whole class that we failed the test. Sometimes its really hard to raise our hand and ask questions. The fear of being told its a stupid question or being laughed at is real, and its kind of terrifying. If you see us struggling, please ask us if we need help. I wish my teachers knew that sometimes we just get tired of school. Sometimes we just really need to sit on the desk or lay on the floor or just take a break for a few minutes. Standing up and talking to our friends or even playing a quick game can make a huge difference. I love to laugh, so please just let us laugh. It's not fair to make us sit in silence for the entire time. I wish my teachers knew that school is hard. We're gonna wanna give up. No matter what, please don't let us give up. I believe that college is for everyone, but not every college is for everyone. Please talk to us about things that we're interested about, or that mean something to us. I wish our teachers knew that life is hard, but we need you in order to succeed.

~

That we are already 2months in school, so lots of teachers are assigning us homework, almost in every class, since i have 3 Ap classes, the assignment are kind of hard, sometime all three AP class give me homework, so it kinda of hard, sometime i wonder, why i'm in these AP classes because i barely understand anything that happen in class, i mean i do pay attention in class, it just that there are some vocabulary that are hard to understand, sometime i don't understand what the teacher is talking about, so it kind of hard to do my assignment sometime. I'm a quite person, i don't like talking out loud in front of the class, i just like to keep it to myself, but i'm working on it, i'm working on talking more in class, like asking questions, and answering them, asking for help instead of just sitting there clueless. I also wish that the teacher understand that the teacher shouldn't teach way to fast, or way to slow, because sometime the teacher would teach something, and then tomorrow there will be a new assignment over something totally different. Sometime there would be days, where i don't feel like doing any works, but i will still do it, because i need to pass this class, and sometime i feel like there isn't enough time in class to do my work, or enough time to finish my homework at school, since i have to go to a different school after this school, so i don't really have enough time to do my work at home. So i think the teacher should expand a little more time so i can do my work, instead of rushing on it every time, because i think the purpose for homework is to learn something by myself at home, so i need time to think, and brainstorm, instead of rushing on it, and just worry about finishing it on time, rather than learning. Sometime even if i'm feel blue inside, or not feeling well or anything, just know that i will come to class on time, and still do my work, even if i'm not ok. The only time i won't do anything is on the test, when i'm not feeling well, i want to have sometime, because i want to pass the test, if i'm not feeling well, i know i will just rush on the rest, and not caring if i fail or pass, because i don't feel like doing my test when i'm not feeling well, because i'm not giving all my effort into it, so whatever that score i got on my test, just know it not from my effort, it just me rushing it so i can finish it early. The thing i want you to do is, to let us review anything that is on the rest, before the day of the test, because we all are human, we will forget something that was said from yesterday, so i think the teacher should review the things that will be on the test, or the teacher should give us a packet, to review over the things, we have learn, so we can study the night before the test, i heard people said, you can memorize more if you study before you sleep, it will help you remember what you have learn, so i think the teacher should do that. I don't know what else to say, my favorite color is red, i like eating papaya salad. I'm a quite person, that doesn't love to talk out loud in front of the class, i'm a independent person, even if i pay attention, i still wont get what the teacher is teaching or saying, sometime i get off track, so yeah. I just want you to know that i don't know why i'm in these AP classes because i feel like i don't belong in here, because sometime i feel like whatever the teachers is teaching, i'm like over here, all space out, and not knowing anything, while the other kid are doing totally fine with their work. So yeah, i really want to know why i'm in these AP classes. My real name is *(full name redacted)*, everyone call me *(name redacted)*, but when i was a kid, my parent doesn't know any english, so they said pronounce my name to one of the people there, so they spell it wrong. *(name redacted)* is not my last name, it is *(name redacted)* and *(first partial name redacted)* and *(second partial name redacted)* is suppose to be together, not apart, so when teacher call me, they be calling me *(first partial name redacted)*, and i'm like here not knowing that they called me, and i would get in trouble, because they be like, you don't pay attention or listen to me take role, that why you didn't hear me call your name, i never argue with a teacher before, sometime the teacher will get on my nerves, because they will be saying stuff that not true, but i don't argue back, because if i did argue back, they will think i'm lying, and i will get in more trouble, sometime i just let them think wrong. I feel like the teacher should ask the student the reason why they are doing this and that instead of yelling and getting to conclusion, instead of knowing why your students is doing this and that, that why sometime the students talk back, because they get blame for something they didn't even do or think they didn't do it. So i think the teachers should talk it out before getting to conclusion. Sometime before the teachers say "NO" ask the students for reason and stuff like that instead of giving straight answer to them.

~

That I barely talk to anyone in here and that I dislike some people in here and I have my reasons. I don't like being in groups with people that's why I'd rather work alone by myself. I'm sensitive and my mood changes real quick, that's why I have a mean look when you see me because my mood changes. I also wish that my teacher knew if someone gets an attitude with me or if I'm talking and they interrupt I'm going to say something back because that's disrespectful. At the time I can be friendly and work with some people but that's only sometimes. I'll only work with people that I feel comfortable with if not I'll just work individually. I have really bad anxiety and when I'm not in the mood I don't want anyone talking to me. I feel like I'm trying to change my attitude because I have a bad attitude. Me having a bad attitude won't get me anywhere in life, it'll just get me in trouble and it'll just worse and worse so I don't want my teacher to worry about my attitude because I'm trying my best to change. I don't like participating in class activities because it makes me go into a bad mood as well but I love English class so I'm just trying to grade up. I'm trying to graduate and get out of Kc because there isn't anything good for me here anymore so once I graduate I'm out of here for sure. I'm also going to move in with my best friend, both of us are already saving up our money so we can start getting everything ready. We're graduating together so me and her are going to make it big. Me and my best friend are also planning to adopt a child when we get older and when we're ready for it. I'm a shy girl, but once you get to know me I have an amazing personality and I make people laugh. I'm actually really outgoing and I like to have fun. I keep my circle small so I only talk to 2-4 people that's it because you never know when they'll switch up and turn fake. When you have more friends it's just drama because that's what mostly everyone likes to do. I like to play volleyball, I was going to join the team this year but I changed my mind and I decided not to join in. I also love to sleep and watch horror movies. The teacher at this school who always motivates me is Sergeant , he always tells me everyday to do better and to just keep doing what I'm doing and I'll make it. I have a lot going on at home that's why my grades keep getting lower because I can't concentrate when all I have on my mind is what is happening at home. I'm trying my best to keep my grades up and to do all my work. My favorite movie is Freedom Writers, it taught me a lot and it's a really good movie. My second favorite movie is Enough, it taught me that you should never let a man put his hands on a woman and that's right because no man should ever do that. They'll be known for putting their hands on a woman. My teacher should also know that I don't think bullying is right, bullying other people makes the other person want to commit suicide and if I was to ever see someone getting bullied I would stand up for that person and I would try to stop it. Nobody deserves to be bullied by another person, and if a person ever told me that they needed something or if I saw someone in the streets who needed something I would buy them something. Some people are just rude and they don't even try to do anything. I'm a lovable person when it comes down to something serious. Like I said earlier I have a bad attitude and my mood changes quick I can also be nice and try to help the people that need it.

~

I wish my teacher knew everything about me. I was born (*date redacted*) in (*location redacted*). I was born at (*time redacted*) and I weighed (*weight redacted*). I usually have a lot of stuff on my mind and sometimes i'm usually depressed. Everyone tells me that my life is easy since i'm rich and all of that. But the truth is that my life isn't easy. I still get punished and I still do my chores. I'm just like everyone else and I'm proud to be like that. I love being who I am as a person. There are some people that don't like me and honestly that doesn't bother me. I like being who I am cause it's who I am.

    I'm not the drama type of person. I like to help people out with their problems. I like to be there when someone needs someone to vent to or a shoulder to cry on. But, sometimes I feel like I don't matter. I hate it when my friends try to change me or disrespect me like it wouldn't matter. They always thought that I was this good person who is sweet, kind, and gentle. But, sometimes I can't always be like that especially if someone is rude to me or family or even my friends.

It just makes me so mad and upset. I don't want my friends to treat me differently. I want them to accept me for who I am. You have to like yourself for others to like and accept you for what you are. The one thing that irritates me the most is when girls or guys talk about who they are dating. I love to see people fall in love, but I hate it when they rub it in your face. I like to stay true to myself.

I will at a point say things to people that will make them feel hurt or angry. I won't mean it when I say something about someone. I don't like to be mean to people but when you make me mad or upset then I will be mean about it. I usually can control my anger but if it gets out of hand then usually I'll just walk out of the room so I can control myself.

I would like to go to college after high school. I either want to be a Marine Biologists or like a song writer or even a lawyer. I love to look at sea animals and just learn about them. I would love to see what they eat and what they do. I love to write new songs. Everyday I will go to my room and just start to write music about anything.

I love to debate and i'm really good at arguing when it comes to proving a point about anything. I like to see the different sides of the debate. A lot of people think that I would be great at debating. I've gone to a lot of schools and I've been going to a lot of places for vacation. 2 of the places I've been to is Texas and Mexico last winter break.

I loved Texas and Mexico. They are awesome places to visit and go like sight seeing. In Mexico there's like a huge population there. There are a lot of food areas and like malls to go to. They have different type of money and it's really amazing to look at different cultures and like what they do. Mexico is just amazing and I actually wish I was able to go back there to relive all of my memories. I had such an awesome vacation there and I will go back over the winter time. This is all that I want my teacher to know about me and I hope you enjoyed reading this.

~

how much students are really going through. I wish that they could take a class that would help them identify the pain and hurt there is underneath a smile. So many undergo students depression at such a young age . This makes them think in a different mentally and prevents to exceeding the full potential. Now days it's so easy to fake happiness simply because others don't care enough to see if you really are doing okay. So many dark thoughts creep into one's mind. Unwanted thoughts and we try to ignore them but it's hard. It's hard to get up each and every time your knock off your feet because you don't have time to get up. You keep getting hit over and over again without end. School is stressing enough that students still have to go home and help their families. Students get recognition for making honor roll or for perfect attendance. What about rewarding those students who work double shift to keep their families of the street. School is much more than it seems. Its an escape from reality , a place where you can be someone else without others knowing. Students are judge about everything: from the way the talk to the way the dress but not from their peers but by themselves. A thought that if you don't fit in why bother. Ever wonder why the kid in the back never raises their hand? It's not because they don't know the subject or they're not smart but because they simply stopped caring. Without a motivation a student won't accomplish anything. Ever wonder why the girl in math class is always done first or doesn't do her work? Maybe just maybe it's not challenging enough. Maybe she's tired of being given such easy work, if you'd challenge her she could be even smarter . Maybe one day she could be a Major in Finance. Run her own company and encourage others to follow their dreams. So stop and think is this what you want for your students failure? Cause that's what you're putting them up for. Some students need to be more challenged while others need to be talked and walked through the process. Some just want more details about the assignment because they want to do it correctly not because they don't understand it. There's so much pressure in being a good student, good athlete and good daughter. Yes we wanna make our parents and teachers proud. But we also wanna do what we like. I believe teachers should get together and create a class where students are allowed to be up instead of just sitting for the whole hour. Give them longer breaks and maybe they wouldn't disrupt the classroom as much. Give students the chance to explore and discover. I also think the district should add a class that helps students figure out what they wanna do for a living. Where they can decided if they wanna go to college or not. We should also have the opportunity to interact with the "REAL WORLD". Students aren't gonna use the distance formula , parallelograms in the real world unless they are studying that. The should offer classes that let teach students how to apply for a job how to file taxes or what's required to buy a house . This is what we really need, because you guys say you're preparing us for the real world but you're really not . You guys are only preparing us for college , for more school but not the actual world. So stop and think what do you want for your students? How can you help your students in a way that can actually help them? Because we can say okay we'll think about it or okay it won't happen again but it's just lies. Actually do something to help us be where we need to be not where we think we need to be or where we want to be.

By (*name redacted*), "A student who wants more and can't settle for less"

Some only settle for what they get while others don't settle at all
Others search for more because
They can't exceed their full potential because it's never ending
They hungrily search for more taking in whatever they can
Just like a bird
if you don't teach it how to fly correctly
How do you expect it to spread it wings and soar
Soar above all
And if you fall get back up stronger than before
Never settle for less when you're worth much more

~

I am 16 years old. I have 6 brothers and 1 sister. I was born in (*place redacted*). moved to (*place redacted*) for my years of 2-4. Then I moved to Northeast Kansas City Missouri and have lived here since 5 years old. Weird fact is the first time I went to school was age 10 in third grade crazy right. I went to (*school name redacted*) from 3rd to 4th grade. Thats where I met my girlfriend in 3rd grade. I got expelled from there permanently. After that my church put me on a scholarship to go to (*school name redacted*) a private school in (*place redacted*). I went there from 5th to the the third day of school 8th grade and then the church said i couldnt go anymore because i left the school and walked across the street without permission so stupid but whatever my life is way better here than there. After that i did not go to school my whole entire 8th grade year because of shot record stuff. Then the place i moved to my girlfriend lived by and we started going out as of September 12 2015 and still going. She went Northeast Middle but I could not get in because of shot records. After that I went to Northeast Highschool my freshman year and now my sophomore year. In the summer of 2016 I got my first job at worlds of fun which was one of the best things that happen to me because when you're young growing up in the ghetto and you work and have your own money you have a sense of freedom you can buy the things you like and do the things you want. Worlds of fun was one the best things because im a very hard worker at 15 years old i was only making 7.75$

and hour not much but through hard work and dedication i got promoted to a supervisor my 2017 season and now when i was working full time in the summer i was making 11.25 and pulling 1000-1400 dollars checks every other friday at just 16 years old i would say thats a huge head start in life. Now granted the fact that i dont really have a life besides work and school it hards because im making a lot of money but im not enjoying my childhood its going away in a flash but at the end of the day i care about the money more and i would be a lot happier with money then to be broke. I do care about my girlfriend very much and my favorite things to do is spend time with her over anything. But when im working and i have all this money to go places and have fun with her i can never find the time so i would say im a pretty busy person and pretty mature. I dont worry about what everyone else is doing i worry about me and what im doing now to reflect what happens in the future. Im not trying to be like all these other kids who skip class and pull d and fs because though some of those people may be very popular. They will also be very unsuccessful to so im gonna stay focusing on school and work and the my girlfriend i gave up basketball and boxing and working out to take care of my he priorities i need to whuch can be very stressful at times.

~

I have no life after school because my family mostly like to stay inside the house and watch tv and eat food.there is some interesting thing that i might do.i have a small farm where i grow some vegetable and me being only eating fresh food is a great way for me to be healthy.my father and i mostly do the manly stuff like fixing the house and fixing car.i also like playing game it help my mind be at ease when thing get tough.i also like playing soccer and basketball even tho i'm not great at basketball however i am great at soccer i played defender for the northeast highschool team it hard making it to every practice.i have a very hard time talking or making new friend because i am mostly shy to people i'm not use to.im know to be the funny guy on a group of friend.i also like to watch drama,movies and skite but i'm mostly into comedy romance movies.i been a very shy and scared person my whole life and most of my friend know that i don't get into fight as most kid do i usually avoid fight before it escalate into physical fight.i love all kind of animal and i love how they live.i hate scary movies because it boring and doesn't excite me much because it funny how they don't run,trip over air and how they do the most stupid thing they could ever do. I like video game mostly fps(first person shooter) it help calm me down or in some cases bring rage and anger to me when i die in the game.I mostly like to swear when i talk to my friend i don't know why but it became so natural to me and i need to stop swearing because my mouth alway get me in trouble.i been working very hard to control my mouth and to control what i say.i dont have the best personality but i do have a kind heart.it sometime difficult for me to say no to someone when they ask me for anything i alway end up giving up and giving it to them.that is why i have no life after school.

~

What I wish my teacher knew is that I'm trying my best. I'm having some personal things going on at home right now. It's kinda stressful. I'm doing my best to try and not let it interfere with my schooling. But it's a little difficult when it's right there in the back of your head nagging you on all day. And other stuff. I've missed quiet a few days this school year already. I'm trying to make up all that work plus get done the new assignments that have be given as well. ~~I'm going to~~ Work has been okay. McDonalds. isn't the best job, but at least for a minor I have a job. Most kids my age don't work. And its hard to find jobs for kids under 16. But I'll be having my sweet 16 soon, so they'll be more job opportunities soon. My Sweet 16 is gonna be great. I'm driving to Lincoln to pick up my best friend and get a few of my other friends together and just do what we do. We might go to the Movies or bowling. Something like that. Have fun and just chill. ~~I'm thinking~~

I'm thinking about ~~doing~~ ~~an~~ going to a hospital and help out/volunteer there. Get into the setting because for future stuff I want to be a nurse annesthesiologist. Thats like one of the highest level nurses. They help out by like putting people to sleep

before they go into surgery and who wake them up after surgery.
This past summer a few weeks before school had started I had surgery on my stomach. And the way the nurses acted and helped and everything inspired me to be like them. I want to be able to help people. Next year I had signed classes at Pinn Valley for Nursing. To get a head start on things.

My cousins and aunt showed up unexpectedly from Florida. It was good to see them, but also stressful. It would have been better if they'd given us a heads-up that they were coming. But all-in-all it was an okay thing.

I have a field trip tomorrow so I won't be in school. We're going to a play. Then afterwards we're going to eat. We won't be here at school until after 6th hour.

My bestest friend since 5th grade is engaged now and is going to be getting married in 2K19. And she asked me to be her maid of honor. I'm so excited and happy for her. Plus her fiancé is a good guy who has a job and is very kind. She did real good. I'm proud of her.

Oh my god!!! Did you hear about all the Kardashian's ~~pregnancies~~ being pregnant. Like all at the same time. Like, but why? Anyway there's always drama with them.

My oldest sister is also engaged. I was there for the proposal. It was cute. She was crying and everything. I'm happy for them. They're really cute together. They are like couples goals.

-Sixth Hour-

I wish my teacher knew she made the class more interesting and i'm proud that they come everyday trying to teach us something new, I don't know how they put up with our ignorant attitudes.I know they feel all that stress.

~

I wish my teacher knew how much work it is to do and keep up everyday. The hours feels longer than forever. It is hard to get your grades up if you having trouble doing it alone. Sometimes teachers don't try to help you with your work or at least talk it out with you. Some teachers want to talk bad on students and put them down instead of lifting them up to become better. We want to succeed and become something. We want to graduate on time instead of being behind things to graduate. I want to be capable to focus in class without being distracted, go to class on time without being late, and also keep my grades to A & GPA up also so I can be able to graduate at least early. I want to be able to get a good paying job and good home to be at without struggling without my diploma. Things get hard at a time because you trying to get finished up at school, have your fun times as much as you can before you don't have it anymore, and you want to be able to take care of yourself in the future. I'm here to get my education and be done and become something my parent didn't get to do. School is really about how much you need to know in order understand in the real world because the things you learning are helpful on how you talk and how you understand people as well as reading a lot of papers to sign. School is the most important thing because the more you push it instead of giving up the more you will achieve you goal. It's a few times I wanted to give it but I made it this far and why would I want to give up now. It's all on how you want to proceed in life and the most thing is don't let your education take the best of you cause you need it more than anyone else do. Look at the people who wish they was in school to stay focus, not be late, or be class clowns in school but instead they didn't succeed in school to become instrudary. I'm pushing myself more into school everyday as much as i can because I two years left and i want keep going until I reach my goal. I want to graduate and become something unique & successful in life.

~

What I wish my teacher knew is how much pain I go through each and everyday with my depression and anxiety. I have a lot of trust issues with people and myself but when I draw I can be myself or when I sing. Also I have a big family so I have a hard time keeping up with my homework and my grades and I am constantly worried about my friends and family sometimes I might look happy but really I am dead inside and today I am feeling really down and all so I might not work my best. Also I am tired of people telling me how i should dress or wear my makeup it really drives me crazy. There are some days where I just want to die and leave this cruel world. Other days I am happy cause I have the people I love and the people who love me. I live in a loud house so that is a lot of headaches and migraines. But I am glad for the people I have in my life who love me so much and I love them as well. Right now I feel like breaking down and crying because there is so much pain in my heart and in my mind I am mentally and emotionally tired. I am so tired of everything in this world and I hate Donald Trump I hope we get a better president soon. I just wanna go to sleep and never wake up. But also I wish I had powers to get rid of all the pain and destruction in this world that is hurting so many innocent people. Also I like writing fairytale stories but I wanna be a attorney and in the army when I get out of school. I hope that when I get older I marry the right person and I also don't wanna have kids when I get older so I hope that my life goes well. My favorite movie is the Hunger games series cause I feel a deep connection to Katniss Everdeen cause she cares for a lot of people and she has so much love for her bestfriend Gale Hawthorne and she loves her husband Peeta meliark that she was willing to die for him in the arena. I also love the show Shadowhunters to me honestly Jace on of the main characters has a really strong out going ego and can be stubborn sometimes but he cares about so many people and not only that I honestly think he is cute. But, Jace he cares for clary and loves her very much and he gets so jealous when she is around other men that is. Jace is a strong shadowhunter he is raised but the best shadowhunter family and has the best family Alec and Lizzy will fight till the end of time for Jace. And Jace and clary fight strong together and they have an angelic bond that lead them right to each other they we made for each other and according to the Fans of Shadowhunters clary and Jace might be Gods or something close to it which drives the fans crazy. If I could be anything I would be a shadowhunter like them. Clary and Jace are my favorite couple out of all the couples in the show I think they should keep them together. But clary is still learning about her angelic powers and so is Jace and Clary has a brothers she never knew about.

~

I wish my teachers knew that sometime how they teach i might not understand. I wish my teachers knew i might not always have a good day or feel happy about coming to school.

I wish my teacher understands what happening at home and what i'm going through.
I wish my teachers knew i don't feel safe in my own school because of bully.
I feel bad sometime because teacher disrespect me and don't wanna listen to what i have to say.
It not fair for student like us to be in this kind situation because the teacher don't care about he or she eduction.
My hobbie is to do business and like making money
I like to buy stuff for a cheap price and resell it to someone might be interesting to buy my stuff and i can sale it a different price and twice more then what i bought.
I like to experience how life is like when you are on your own with your own responsibility without any body help it hard on your own to have a lot a responsibility but it life.
I Am a person who like to be independent i don't want any help from anybody especially my family because my parent have help me all my life and i wanna gave them back everything they have provided me.

I wanna take care of my parent when they get older i wanna provide them anything i can to assist them and i would never put my parent in a nursing home because they don't deserve to live in those kind of imvironments because they rise you to be independent person.
If you have a kind hearts you would never leave your parent somewhere you don't wanna end up there to.

I wish everybody love each other in my family because i don't feel that love from siblings i wish we was in one peace and don't argue and fight.

~

I wish my teacher knew that I shoot 100 shots a day and practice dribbling for an hour. Sometimes i have really busy nights and i'm gonna sleep in class sometimes. I wish my teachers knew that the work they give us is not the most important thing in the world and they wouldn't be on my back so much about it. I wish teachers would understand that we are at school around our frans and that we are gonna laugh joke and play together. I wish teachers would understand that if i see a girl i like then i'm not gonna do nothing until i go talk to her and see wats da deal wit her. I am the g.o.a.t of basketball I can rap ima good worker i'm funny i like to make ppl laugh i'm the best person in the world to be around you are guaranteed to laugh no doubt i like school because after you are done wit school you are not gone be in a super big building filled wit girls my favorite rappers is 21 Savage, lil uzi vert, famous dex aka dexter, and kodak black i feel like i am the best basketball player in the world and i'm getting better and better everyday my biggest goal right now is to make the basketball team. School, Basketbal, Girls, Money and Family are the most important things in my life right now. I REALLY NEED HELP WITH GETTING A JOB. I tried all summer to get a job but i didn't get 1 so i spent most of my summer cutting grass and at the basketball court and at church. I got swag yea i got that sauce i be lookin fresh every time i walk in the school.

~

I wish my teacher knew how hard i worked just to get to this point in life because high school is tough and i got to keep my grades up & GPA and get my credits to graduate high school to become something big in my life. Some teachers do care and some don't but that doesn't matter. What matter's that i need to pass the 9th grade. I love to play football and run. My favorite nfl team is the New York Giants. Favorite player is Odell beckham Jr. because he's a big role model on and off the football field. My biggest goal is to make it to the NFL because i have to skill & Mindset to accomplish it.

~

i wish my teacher knew i want to succeed . i want to graduate , get a job , start my own business or have a new relationship . thinking of these goals brings me positive feelings and emotions because i know that my life plans are fulfilling and that i'm making visible progress . i wanna succeed , i wanna look back and be proud of myself . i wanna walk across the stage and make my family happy . i wanna prove people that doubted me wrong . achieving my success is a positive experience . it adds value to me and pumps my ego . achieving success to me is like a personal victory. i love winning . its like when two children play a game they both want to win. it doesn't matter if there is a prize. i don't need a purpose . it's in my deep nature to want to win and thats what im gonna do . i'm gonna succeed .

~

I wish my teacher knew how hard I overthink a lot of things. We could get an easy assignment and i would think the most out of it and sometimes i would not even do it because of how much i know it will/would stress me out. I wish my teacher knew that i like working but for some reason i just don't put effort in trying, I think about doing something but i either get distracted or just forget. At home it feels like i'm a mom too because I have to care for my younger family members and that's distracting too. I want to get a job but i already know that would stress me out too. I don't know why i don't walk the extra mile for trying to do my work i think i lack motivation i think if i was really motivated i would probably try harder, i also think one of my big distraction is my phone i try to not use it as much but i always have it close to me so i decide to just use it because I'm usually bored anyways. I really want to be successful but i know if i keep on being like this i won't get anywhere. I think if somebody just came up to me and told me "you got this today" or said some motivational thing to me, id try because that would make me think that someone actually has faith in me. I don't hate school i think, because it's a place where you can make friends and make new experiences and learn mistakes. I just don't like how some things go down you know? I feel like if someone were to drop out or something like that, they'd miss school because being at home doing nothing gets boring unless you're out making money living life or whatnot but I've learned from people in my family. I really hope i'm the first one to graduate in my family i think that would make everyone happy and all but the person i would most likely do it for is my mom because she's been with me through it all and she's such a hard worker and i love her for that. I think life is about taking risks because honestly you do only live once and you have to make the most out of it like if you see a cute stranger and you feel like you're too shy or you fear rejection just say f*** it and go for it because you'll probably only see that person once so it really doesn't matter if you make a fool out of yourself. I think the world is cool to be honest like the ocean and stuff and so many places that are undiscovered, it's just all fascinating how we're all literally living on a floating rock in space, that should really make you think. I want to travel and see many places in the world and pet so many animals but then my thought goes again to school and how im not determined on working hard, maybe that should be my motivation, but it's funny because even if i still had that thought in my head i would still probably fail, I'm very forgetful like i forget a lot of things and that makes me mad

~

I wish my teacher knew that school was tough because school is not easily you got to had good grades. For all your work to be turned into graduate. Sometimes i well like i am going to fail cause i got a couple of bad grades in this class. And i turned all my work in for this class. But in the rest of my grades in all my other classes are good. And im proud of myself that they are good and that i am in the 12th grade.to be honest i thought i would never make it this far too. The 12th grade. I love school it means alot to me and i am going to be upset when i graduate im going to miss all of my favorite students. That i really liked alot. But i just feel like i am going to fail this class but my teachers tell me that i am fine and i will still graduate. There are some subject i do not understand in classes some assignments are hard for me. And some are easy but i just don"t like.asking for help from my teachers i am just a shy person. But i need to focus on all my classes and study more. And start asking my teachers for help more. Then my grade would be a lot better in this class. Maybe i can ask my mother to help me like she can be my study buddy or ask me questions and see if i can get it right. Now i live at a shelter and i do not like living their my mother can"t afford a place right now but she is working and my favorite color is red and i love dogs favorite dog breed is pitbulls. I have 3 brothers and 3 sisters im the 6th oldest and the last child is my brother and he goes to the same school at me then i am a uncle but i Don"t see my nieces or nephews. And they mean a lot to me. I love gaming and i love hanging out with my sister and my brother in law i love playing video games with him. I have 5 cousins 4 are older than me one is the same age as me and one is younger than me. My favorite sport is football and basketball. My favorite football team is the dallas cowboys and the chiefs. Thats who i love. Then my favorite basketball team is golden state warriors. I love cartoon movies also. My favorite cartoon is tarzan. And lorax i love horror movies also. I love stephen kings it and misery pet sematary and kujo them are stephen king movies one one is horror i believe and i like the chucky movies also. I love four wheeling with my friends and i love to hang out with friends also. I am just a active person i love to walk every where. I like spending time with my mother a lot on her days off from work she only works on the weekends thats all she does is work to make money but only on the weekends and thats it she works on week days some times when they call her in and they ask her too come in for work. But i love being asround everybody. Favorite kind of food is mexican food and chinese food i love hot wings breakfast for dinner like biskits and gravy. I love too wrestle with my oldest brother and younger brother also they are fun to wrestle with and to get a lot with. I get along with my family sometime but not all the time. They are my world and i love them so i wouldn"t know what to do without them if i lost them.

~

what i would be doing throughout the days. How hard it would be. Coming home to " go clean this . or go get me this from the store" being asked to go get the clothes from the drier. Going outside in the night time. To see if my dogs have food for the night and morning. And if they did not have food i would have to be going upstairs struggling to open a door that i try to open with all my force and all. Deciding what to wear for tomorrow. Now washing clothes.

Then going outside to help my dad with construction then come back in for a minute break and then take him a big cup of cold ice water. Waiting til we finish, waiting for him to go tell me to take all the stuff up this drive thru that has a really big hill. Having to take in all of the cement machine then running back down to now take the shovel and scooper to all the way upstairs. Now having to help feed my dad. And my brother although he is old enough to make his own food for himself but hes just so lazy. Then having my brother come into my room and mess up my whole room. Then he would get out of the front room and leave it a mess and leave the door wide open when he would leave with his friends. Now there is me having to clean up his candy wrappers , tissue, and all his mess that he leaves around the house. Now having to go fix my room, remake my bed all over again bc he jumped on it.

My favorite hobby is going outside and playing soccer. And walking my dog. The reason i like soccer is because as a kid i used to like to kick things a lot so i would have to just grab a soccer ball or any kind of sports ball and kick it against my wall. Outside and then i grew up watching soccer. Going to the park with my brother and his friends being a goalie and then aiming towards the net. Last year well in 9th grade. I joined soccer and i had alot of fun. Actually playing in games. Making new friends and everything having a great time. With everyone. Especially when my friend or the striker would make a goal. Another reason i like it is because i can get all my stress out on the ball and being able to just let everything go and be free and just being able to do what i like. I like going to take my dogs on walks because i can go take him for walks. And being able to go explore things. I have this dog his name is " oso" he is a full blooded german shephard he is white. So a lot of people think that he is mixed with something else. But he is my favorite dog. He is like a best friend alothough they said its only a mans best friend. But he is like my best friend i tell him everything although i dont get a responds but when i need someone to talk to just let it out hes always there. If im sad or crying he would come and check up on me. Hes is very protective too. My favorite food is chinese and tacos . the reason i like chinese food is because i am just in love with it i like fried rice and all this other type of food. Tacos are the best. MY favorite is tacos de carne asada. All the other types of flavors and others are kinda nasty or just dont have a taste.

My birthday is on (*date redacted*) . my favorite color is blue and purple and red.

My favorite shoes are vans and converse. I had a quinceanera. Last year on the (*date redacted*) and it was really good everything had went out well and all. I had 7 damas and 7 chambelans. I miss those days. all my friends would come over to my house and we would all practice the steps for dancing and all. They would always come over every day around like 7 or 7 30. The day before my quince we went to the hall and we went to go decorate it and had fun and all. But the big day had finally came. I woke up at 5am to go take a shower and then i went to go take a shower and then after i couldnt blow dry my hair. But the hair dresser style lady or what ever she was. Came at 6 to do my make up and my hair. I was so nervous but half asleep. And then after ward my friend had came upstairs and all . she had slept over and all the day before and the day after. She had ccame up and we took pictures after the lady had finished doing my hair. Then after that we went downstairs into my moms room well just me and my mom and she helped me put on my dress and crown and shoes. Then we had waited for everyone

~

Tbh i wouldn't want my teacher knowing anything about my life because it seems like when teachers interfere with children's lives things get worse. I don't why i think they think it's their job but sometimes you should just leave well enough alone. It's a good thing they wanna help and sometimes you can and sometimes you can't but this is really only the case when a student has a stressful lifestyle but i would want my teacher to know that i do try my hardest in class no matter what mood i'm in and i don't like asking for help sometimes even when i need it. I don't like school very much it's not teachers or the classes it's the other students that make me hate in a particular class the students are always loud and never listen. Someone always is about to fight or arguing since the first day of school it's been like this and not once has there been a chill day where everyone is just calm i shouda passed it last year when i had the chance but i'm happy is only for one semester. I really don't know what i wanna be ,i mean i do but i don't 1 of the 3 a judge a vet or a children's doctor. I love animals and children and i wanna help my fellow people that is why i wanna be these things i just wish i could be all three i use to think i could, go to school to become a judge then work a lil then go to school and be a vet. Or i thought i could go to school for each one, one after the other and then when im done and i have my degree to be a judge,vet and a doctor i can do whichever one i want to or all

~

I wish my teacher would know that life is good theres up and downs but recently my dog died so that was kinda sad but everything dies. Im looking forward to homecoming and having fun also my families taking me and my boyfriend to the haunted house Saturday im kinda scared because last time i went it was scary and im also scared because my bf has heart problems and he cant handle to much jump scares so im kinda worried about him but im sure he'll be okay. Schools been the same having a little trouble with math but im getting better my grades are looking good it sucks i have to take algebra 1 over again but honestly i needed it. My sister just had a baby a few weeks ago im happy about that but not happy that her other little demon is gonna get jealous that shes not the baby no more. Im also looking forward to freakers ball. Freakers ball is a big rock concert and one of my favorite singers are the headline Marilyn manson and im more than exiced. For halloween ill stay home with my mom and invite my bf over to hand out candy and my dad will go down to our bar well also my dad owns a bar called Club tanqueray. Recentlly ive been obsessing over Dr. pepper like i might be addicted i crave it all the time but then i searched up if Dr. pepper gives u acne and well it does but i dont care ill survive!

As a person im a very picky eater i dont like to much fruit and i only like 3 vegitables. I enjoy spending time with my friends, family and bf. I love going to the newest scary movies i love horror movies but my bf hates them but he watches them with me! I really wanna see the movie Happy Death Day it looks good but i think the killer looks lame why are scary movies going down hill? Like why cant stuff be good like hellraiser or friday the 13th and even pumpkin head? But i think they shouldnt remake scary movies like It because they really dont make it good like the remake of it was "okay" but in my opinion not as good as the orginal. Well thats just me. Welllll people are just judging i see people are the school and people look at how they act or wear but everyones different but i guess some people dont get that. I think people should never be judged for being themselves. Hmm recently ive been obsessing over this band called My Chemical Romance and its really a good band and my french teacher always asks me about them and he puts there music on for the class even though they dont like that type of music. I think its a nice thing to do!

~

I wish my teacher knew how hard it is for me to get to school.

~

It is to do and keep up everything and. The hours is for every class and help you to do other work so you won't have to stay in the same room for 7 hrs it's so easy to move to different classes and do diff work and i am happy to move classes everyday because it's so much easier to do everyday and, its longer . but, it would take forever to stay in the same class everyday and boring to see the same teacher and just sit there and listen and do the same work , but there is some people out there that wants to stay in the same class and do the same work and just be bored and see the same teacher and just listen to the same teacher but, there is a lot of students out there that likes switching classes everyday accept the weekends . im proud of being in this school because it's fun and cool looking and the lunch room is different and we do different things together all the time in my other classes . what it's like a home with my grandparents and dad and my animals it's greatful and awesome and wonderful and i love being with my grandpa and my nana and my dad and my animals to be honest though i would love a different place with them then it would be better. My favorite subject in school is math and World history it's easy because all you have to do is to copy stuff down and city year helps us a lot and everyday with everything. Sometimes i hate school when i don't feel like getting up and feel ,like sleeping all day and don't feel , good and don't feel like going to school . okay my fav sport is volleyball because when i was 10 years old i always wanted to be a volleyball player but, i can't because it's too late to go play now because it already too much girls on the team . about myself i am a really good student and a really good runner for track but, i have asthma though so that's why i ain't in no sports rn i could rn but, i'm scared that i might pass out and faint, but i don't have my inhaler so ya that is why i can't be in sports rn. ?? my dog is dying and her name is diamond . and my papa is too . he has cancer a lot of cancer he's hair is falling out and he has one kidney so saddd???/something else but, i'm not saying he don't want me too it's too embarrassing to him and he wouldn't like me rn if i tell you rn.

~

I wish my teacher knew that I have short term memory loss and I have a hard time thinking. I also have a hard time paying attention when the teacher talks for a while.Sometimes I get tired then I don't want to do the work. When class is long it tends to get boring talking about 1 subject. It's harder for me to learn when everyone has to do their work quietly and the teacher does not work our way through the worksheet. I also wish that the teacher knew that every time I think I don't get any sort of answer. Sometimes school is tough when there is 7 hours of school. People get bored of all the work that's get put onto them. It would be easier if there was 4 hours of school.

Stuff about myself: I have short term memory loss. I love Video Games. I also love YouTube.
When I get older, I'm going to be one of the best YouTubers there is. My other hobby is spending time with my friends. I also love to go to the library and read some anime books. At home our family is having a hard time with bill but we are getting better. I'm trying to work on getting a work permit so I can work at Quiktrip and help with the bills. My dad has 1 lung because his other one broke down on the metro bus on the way to work.

More about me: Sometimes when I go outside is to the library or friends but if I can't do either I just look around at places I've never been. My favorite sport is football because I love to throw the ball and pass it around. My favorite food is Tuna Fish Casserole because the Tuna mixed with macaroni is really amazing. The taste of the cheese is so good. I have 4 sisters living with us 2 brothers and a mom and a dad, with 2 cats. Oe of our other cats died 2 weeks ago. My favorite color is Purple because of this game I like it's call Saints Row and it's one of my favorite games I've played just like GTA 5. I also love to play Call of Duty because of the simulation and the switching sides. Just Like Rainbow Six: Siege. I also love to play Splinter Cell blacklist because it also has a Multiplayer to it and it's the latest Splinter Cell there is.

The other job I might be trying to get is called Vintage Stock, it's a Video Game store and it shows lots of movies games and tv series that people love. It also has lots of action figures in there. When it comes to working I love to listen to music. Listening to music is soothing and it helps your brain out. It also soothes your brain.

~

What i was going through on a daily basis. I have a hard time dealing with my emotions on my own. I have depression, and ive been dealing with it for a long while now. In the time that i've been having it, i havent met anybody that can really understand how/what i'm feeling. All my friends think they know that i'm going through, but i know they don't. It's hard for me to open up to people and tell them what's wrong with me because usually no one really connects with me and comprehends. I hate having to deal with depression on an everyday basis, it causes me to lose focus on school related things. It's always getting in the way of be being successful in school, ive tried many things to overcome it but nothing works. I just wish i could find that one person that i can truly open up to and share my deep feelings to without worrying about them telling someone else. But in this world that i live in, finding someone that trustworthy is impossible. Luckily, i have people that kind of understand what's wrong with me. Besides my depression, i feel that i'm a pretty strong and kind of happy person. I love listening to music, it calms me down whenever i'm worked up or stressed. I love learning new things everyday, no matter what it is i never have a problem discovering things. I absolutely love having deep conversations about life and all the weird, crazy, "supernatural" things that occur. I love making theories about things that havent been scientifically proven. Like, for example, what happens to us when we've passed? Where does our soul go? What does it feel like?. Questions like those really gets my mind thinking. I especially love it when the other person has cool theories about it aswell. Something else i love is family traditions, they make me feel so happy knowing that they keep going on for years and years. One family tradition i really love is a Quinceanera. If you don't know what it is, a quinceanera is a big milestone for latinas. It's when they reach the age of 15, which symbolizes becoming a young woman. They have big parties with big, beautiful, poofy dresses and a court with all of your closes friends. You also have to come up with dances like the ballroom dance with your main chambelan (main man/friend/cousin) and you're court, then after that you have to have a surprise dance. Which is alot of fun. How do i know all of this you might ask? Well because i recently had mine in august.

~

I wish my teacher knew that my hand hurts and i can't write at all. To be honest I don't know what to talk about so Imma Just write something, I wish my teacher knew I liked french fries then maybe she would get me some. 💯 •I wish she knew that McDonald's is my favorite restaurant and I wish she knew this assignment was boring, she lucky i like free writing because I would be sleep right now.. She a pretty cool teacher tbh she chill but sum wrong wimme idk what it is, but imma try to work harder.

I wish she knew I didn't like this school and imma be switching school later on, I want to but I don't at the same time, like I like Northeast Inna way like all my friends go here, but then again i know "EVERYBODY" at East it's my favorite school but i don't know what I wanna do i might go back it might not only time will tell 💯 • I'm just confused right now.

I wish my other teachers knew that my hand hurted too because they at like i'm lying about it or something you can clearly see the swelling and I tried to show them but they don't listen, but imma just go to the hospital so I can get one of those fancy things wrapped around my wrist, I mean it won't do much for me but still imma get it because my wrist do hurt a lot.

School is really boring well sometimes it's pretty cool like how it is right now in this class and that's only because i love writing and like typing a little bit, it's just that I never have anything to write about so I just free write most of the time it comes out good or just average and the teachers say " It's creative", i'll take creative☺, besides i like my creativity.

I wish my teachers knew I didn't like facebook because I like writing and all facebook is acronyms and i don't be knowing what they mean, that's why I write everything full and clean so people actually know what I mean. Not that it matter they'll just shorten it anyways.

~

I wish my teacher new how I have just a sertene change of personality as y I can be happy one minute and get mad at the drop of a dime. I wish she new how my feelings get heart very esily. I wish she new how saying I act different makes me ruder then what I was. And I wish she new how much I love music, Money, and playing around. I wish she new how I don't like when the class isn't laffin. I wish she new my dreams of becomeing a train conducter or a lawyer. I also wish she new how I hate not being active like being still. And I wish my teacher new how important they are to my life and I hope she nows that I like sports like basketball, football, soccer, and baseball. I hope she knows how shy I am about being around people I don't know or that I don't like when people I don't know touching me or when I don't play basketball at my full potinchal or when my friend act like he or she dosen't know, and I hate when me and sister or brother fight or when I had to do estra sturf after I am already done with what I'm sopuset to do. An I don't like when I write and my hand starts shaking becaue I'm writeing to fast.

I wish my teacher new that its hard for me in school. People mock me, they even make fun of me, they trip me in the hallways. I wish my teacher new that I can't get work done on my computer because it distracts me knowing I can get on other sites. I work better on paper because I love to write. I wish my teacher knew that the days I don't come are for personal reasons. I wish my teacher knew that I can't see far, or hear out of one ear. I wish my teacher knew how hard it is to go to school with people that want to fight you and your little sister. I wish you knew sometimes I wanna quit school because of sertain people that was my friends and now you can't stand them. I wish you knew how hard it is to wake up

Knowing you live is a lie. Knowing you want to break down in the bathrooms at school just so kids and teachers don't ask what's wrong. I wish you knew that one day I want to become something big so I can prove everyone wrong of who my mother was. I want to grow up to be someone important. I thought about being a lawyer but know I want to be a writer to tell my story. To tell about what was hard and what was a blessing in life. I wonder how many book I would get published. 1 or maybe even 3. I wonder if you knew how hard I want to pass this class. I wish my teacher knew what I was going through. That's not even hair. You want to know who I am? I am _____. I like to watch movies w/ popcorn, I like to see and learn new things about life.

I want to become a writer and help people become something big. I want to do a good thing when I grow up and help sick people to become their self again. My favorite colors are blue, purple, baby blue, a light purple, and grey, black, yellow. My hobbies are to walk around my block. I like to sleep, watch Youtube. I like to go shopping (when I have money). My favorite singer is Selena Gomez, and My Chemical Romance. Sometimes Three days grace. My favorite type of movie would have to be horror or thriller. My favorite movie is Friday the 13th or Saw II. My favorite thing to do is sleep away all negitive things in life, by that saying is I only think of positive things. That is what I wish my teacher knew. How life goes for me. I just wish life can go good for me when I'm older. I hope I make the right decisions.

I wish my teacher knew how much of a struggle it is to work with others that cause a distraction and how so many people thinks it's okay to treat me like I'm nothing and want to try to come at me for no cause no purpose no nothing. People think that I will be okay just staying by myself but, That's not fair! If I have to work hard and tried to be friendly only to deal wit such crazyness, I might of well be by myself. You see so many people tried so hard to keep it real and to be struggling as a 10th grader, it's difficult. You know I can't be successful when other people around me are not trying to be, it's a little unfair that teachers want to yell at you for the simple things but they knew what we go through to get there then teachers wouldn't say nothing about we don't turn in our work and stuff like that and if I keep struggling with the things I do and what I go through many people will just ask me how did I get through all this problems and still try to make it out on time to school. You see growing up when I was little I was digpose with a speech impediment to the point I can't speak without mumble ing to you what I was saying to you and it's really hard to learn things untill one day god bless my vocals to the point I can speak today without mumbling every word to you. I just so happy that jesus christ saved my life and I shall dewel in the house of the Lord for ever. Now I want to pray. Dear heavenly father, we come again to say thank you for waking me up this morning you didn't have to but you did anyway and I jus want to. Give god the glory and the power for I am blessed and greatly to be praised so to the bottom of my broken heart thank you for being part of my life for you had did such an amazing thing to me and for that I want to praise you in the name of jesus christ amen. I just so tired to be honest and im happy to say I want to go to sleep LOL really badly I just want to go home change and go to sleep for a couple of hours. So with that being said I thank you for hearing me out teacher Thank you.

I wish my teacher knew alot about me. I wish my teacher knew I dont work well with new people, and that I really have a great personility even all of the stress and frustration. I wish she knew how i have alot going on at home and how i dont have any friends, I also wish she knew that i was actually depressed instead of being "fine". I wish she knew why i was always laughing and making jokes not knowing how unhappy I was.

After that, I wish she knew that every once in a while I need a "hug" and a few words of encouragement to keep me going. Next, I wish she knew how hard i was working on trying to graduate from northeast high school, I wish she knew that I wanted to show everybody in my family that I can make it

in life by getting a well paying job and by going to college.

-Seventh Hour-

My life is horrible from the situations im put in or the ones i start its very boring and very tiring

~

I wish my teacher knew
That I'm 6'0 and that I

~

I wish my teacher knew that she's my favorite teacher and that her class is my favorite because this is one of my favorite subjects and also because she's a really good and nice teacher. I think she does a good job at teaching me in this class and this is the only class I actually look forward to because we learn a lot more than just english. We learn a lot about the Government spying on us and stuff like that. We also learned about the 4th amendment and also a little bit about immigrants. She cares about our life outside of school and how we can make ourselves better because she has us write goals for our self and also has us tell her about different parts of our week such as something that made me happy, something that made me mad or sad, something that made me laugh, and also something that I learned throughout the week. She also keeps our lesson interesting by not giving us boring stuff all the time and actually giving us work that's fun to research and learn about like the government spying on us and the 4th amendment. I think she also does a very good job at teaching us and keeping us focused and also being nice enough to help us keep our grades up by fully explaining the work before she gives it to us. So the thing I want my teacher to know is that I think she's a nice teacher and is fair by helping us a lot with our work and by not giving us boring assignments. The only reason I don't like school is because all of my classes are boring but this class is actually fun. It's also fun being able to work on topics that she let's us choose, like on our essay where she's letting us write about what we want instead of making us all write about the same thing like a lot of teachers at this school. I also think it's good how she is not just serious and mean all the time.

~

I want to become an NFL player when I grow up. I have been playing football since I was 6 years old. I started playing because my uncle was the coach for a little league team called the Buffalos, and at first I didn't want to play but my mother made me. When I first went i didn't like it because it was hot and I had to wear some big pads. But after the first game and I got use to it and it was really fun. Then I just started playing it more and now I just love it. I play running back, wide receiver, and tailback on offense, and on defense I play corner, safety, and linebacker. I played for our school for a little at those positions but I couldn't play after the first game because of my grades from last year. My favorite to watch is the New England Patriots, I like them because they have my favorite player Tom Brady. To me Tom Brady is the best Quarterback to ever play in the NFL. I say this because he has been to 7 superbowls and has won 5 also in his latest super bowl he came back from 35-3. I also like julian Edelman and Rob Gronkowski, I like them because I like watching how they play.

~

That she is one of the best teachers I have ever had, I'm not just saying that, I mean it. I like how when one person is acting up she doesn't get mad at the whole class like other teachers. I like how the assignments aren't just busy work, they actually teach me something. I also like how she explains the assignments and actually tries to help us of we need help. I like how her assignments challenging, but not impossible. I like how we do it one section at a time, and day by day, and not trying to cramp a whole section in 50 minutes. I like how she gives us what we need to do her assignments, instead of just giving us half of what we need. I like how she wants her students to be engaged in class work. I like how she cares about her students like no other teacher has since 6th grade. I don't know what to type so I'm gonna just get things off of my mind since this is a free write......I think. Nevermind. I like how she doesn't exclude anyone. I might just be saying all this because english is my favorite subject. But last year it wasn't because the teacher didn't care about our interests, our if we knew what we had to do. Since we have to write the whole time now I'm just gonna type whatever comes to mind. You what would be amazing? If you have a high A, like a 97% in a class but you have a 79% in another. I wish you could give like 2% of your grade to another class, because some of these teachers choose to be rude and have it to where your 1% away from an A or a B. ooooh I'm gonna tell you what I honestly want my future to look like. I honestly wanna become a successful youtuber, who has at least 3 million subscribers. If that's successful, I would wanna buy a house with at least 5 big bedrooms. One for my mom, 2 for my sisters (but the one who treats my like doo-doo right now). Another room for me, and one for filming videos. I wouldn't wanna live with one of sisters because she is honestly dirty and I know that if I have a good amount of spending money she would say to get a housekeeper, but I like to do things like that myself. I would honestly stay in Missouri so that I can be close to my family. I would probably only go to LA if they ask me to be in a movie. I don't if you know this but I honestly have a side dream of becoming an actor. Honestly all my dreams have flaws. LIke I might only get to 100 subscribers, or I might not get any roles, because I don't think my face could fit any roles for a TV show. I think my face could only be in a movie because eventually people would get bored of me. I think I could be in a movie because I honestly see movies and the acting is HORRIBLE, and I could honestly play a 35 year old women than a 35 year old women. If I do get a role i feel like it would be a low budget movie, and I was the only decent actor they could find by last minute for the role. I overheard people saying they wanna be famous and drop out of high school. I think thats the dumbest thing you could do, because fame in unpredictable.

~

I wish my teacher knew is the things i like to do well i like to play games and watch anime and listen to music.music helps me to be calm. My favorite types of music is rap/hip-hop but not the ones that are coming out today that are popular i'm talking the ones that are very lyrical the ones that talk about deep thing but sometimes i like to listen to music with a good beat and bass. I also want my teacher to know that i'm going to be trying my best to do work because my mom came from vietnam for mine and my sisters education to better knowing full well that her dad and mom was sick she left because the education over there costed money and her family was poor so she couldn't go to school herself and she couldn't afford to take us to school and also paying for school and our lunches so she came over here so we can get our education and i feel like i trouble her because when i was kid i didn't understand this and all i did was get in trouble and i would get into fights for no reason what so ever and i would get suspended or put in iss i got into so many fights that i actually got expelled than i had to go to a different school i was in 2nd grade when all this happened than my dad thought it was because it was where i lived and the other kids around me and how my mom and my dad fought to much at home and one day in the 4th grade he came to school to take me the *(place redacted)* here i finished the rest of 4th grade then i stayed there till 6th grade my dad wouldn't let me talk to my mom even on the phone only till friday which i got to go to visit my mom than my dad went to jail for 6 months and my mom came over to take me back after the 6 months i grew on my mom and didn't want to go back after i told my dad this after 1 week after my dad got out he tried to drag me out the house and forced me to go with him which i escaped and went inside and locked the door he did this all when my mom was upstairs sleeping so she came down stairs with my sister we had to get a restraining order on him now i'm here both my dad and mom was never rich because they didn't have high school diplomas so of course they didn't go to college so they both didn't have good jobs to get money but my mom works two jobs now 3 in a couple weeks so she can support us with all the things like clothes, and food and around 3 weeks ago her dad/ my grandpa died so it hurt her very bad i had feelings about it but not that strong because i never met him and i never got to meet my dad's dad nor his mom because his mom died in a house fire before i was born and his dad died of cancer.My dreams are to get a good job to support my mom and give back to her and the people in my life that helped me out. I wanna go to film school because i wanna become a movie producer and also a youtuber at the same time so i can support my mom as the best as i can i wanna buy her all things that she ever wanted in her life i also want to support my dad with things he wants because i know i made him out too look like a bad guy just now by typing all of that but he is a good guy all he wanted was me to succeed and become a good person he was nice to he bought me a lot of things despite him not being able to get a job he wanted me to get a good education and both his parents died his mom died in front of him in a house fire.He cared for me i know this because i went to school a little early and he came home from work and he was looking for me and he was crying he thought someone kidnapped me.

~

I wish my teacher knew the hard times and things going on in my life. I have been through a lot. Moving from (*place redacted*) to Kansas City to (*place redacted*) then back. I have experienced lots of different things. Last year when I left Kansas City is where it all begin. This is when I started to realize how life really is. Everyday for about 2 months I have learned new things that made me stop doing and making not so smart choices. I have never done drugs or drank alcohol. The have been much going on during this time, which would take too much time typing about. Noticing fake friends and fake people. My circle was only a few friends that never switch or turned on me, these friends are the one i liked being around. We would hang out after school doing not so dumb things. Then family problems started to occur. I lived with my three other brothers and also my two sisters. My oldest brother always work from morning to night everyday. Everytime he did have free time he would either be sleeping or mad because he couldn't get want he needed to do done. Then he realized how boring his life was up in this area so he decided to move back to KC. Me, my

mom, my brothers and my sisters didn't want him to leave. He still wouldn't change his mind, so he left. Then a few days later I my other sister moved up in this area from texas. I was pretty happy that this was happening. Things went smooth until me and my other brother started having problems. I'm not sure how we started. But I only had a small circle of friends and I had school work and sports.
To be continued...

~

I wish my teacher knew that at the age of 6 my passion for reading began. I remember being in this program called head start, growing up i always wanted to go to school. When my mother went to sign me up for school they said i was too little, i was only 4 years old and you had to be 5 , my birthday is in october and school started in august if that makes sense , that made me be a year behind. Her friend told her that she signed her son at this program called head start. So my mom went and there i was. I loved going there, we had field trips and by the age of 5 i could read fluently. I remember being ahead of everyone, so my teacher told me to enter this contest called storytelling. That made me fall inlove with books, i would read and read read. In the contest they would read you a book and the one who would put in their own words and acted out would win. It wasn't just a school contest it was a whole district type of thing. In the first year i enter when i was still in head start i didn't win. Which made me sad but i still didn't give up, when i was in kindergarten i decided to try again so i did, as they were calling the names of the people who were going to win, I remember being nervous and sweating. They called in 3rd place and i didn't hear my name. My goal was to be 2nd place, and when they called 2nd place i started to cry because it wasn't my name. When i heard 1st place they shouted out my name. I couldn't believe it, i even looked around because i thought another [person with the same name] got the 1st place. They said my name again one more time and also my middle name that's when i knew that it was definitely me. That's been one of my biggest accomplishments. As i got older i felt like story telling wasn't for me, so i quit. But i still read, my brother would make of me, he would say he would give me a dictionary or an encyclopedia for my birthday or for christmas, which he actually did, when i turned 8 he gave me a dictionary which i still have, it's somewhere in my closet. My favorite kind of books are the one with heartbreaks, the way the authors put so many emotions in words is just something else. I've cried a couple of times while reading, i also dream of writing my own book one day, i just don't know of what, maybe my middle school experience, changing locations i really don't know but it will be interesting i promise. I also like poetry, Rupi Kaur is one of my favorite authors, and i feel like there's no one like her. She showed me the meaning of life . Her first book is called milk and honey, it touched my heart She's coming to kansas city on oct. 13 and i cannot wait the best part is that you're getting her new recent book for free, which is called the sun and her flowers, seeing her in person would really make my heart warm. I also hope to get a picture with her.

~

I wish my teacher knew that i think school is not so tough, just the reasons why I don't sometimes come to school is because back in elementary school I dealt with a lot at home so I wasn't really at school as much and it became a habit. Sometimes i just want isolate myself from others and just be alone to set myself straight again, even when i'm alone i feel like everyone is against me for some reason and i start to get anxiety, my mom thinks it's depression since she suffers from it, she tells me my symptoms are the same like hers but that's something people don't get. My life for me now feels way much better than how it used to be back then, back then my life was so terrible I dealt with a lot of family problems, school problems, that's why now i'm so shy, quiet, and nervous now. I wish my teacher knew that I like school, i don't think it's boring whatsoever I just think it's tough because of the things i go through every now and then. I finally learned how to stay to myself and how to work on myself when i'm feeling some sort of way. I wish my teacher knew that sometimes I want to cry for no apparent reason and how hard it is to hold in tears in school. I also wish my teacher knew that these thoughts that go through my head distract me so much from learning, it's like i'm in a whole different world. I want my teacher to know that i want to become someone successful, i want to be the first from my family to graduate high school, get a good paying job, i want to become a veterinarian and help out animals because the love I have for animals is really real (I have 10 dogs) but I also want my teacher to know that even though I get sad/distracted during school/class that I still try regardless, it doesn't hurt to try. I don't get all the support from my parents and friends but I know they want me to have a bright good future so I try to push myself to go to school, do my work and everything else i need to do. I really want my teacher to know that I feel comfortable with letting her know half of my struggles and why i am the person i am today. I love to write, i can literally fill up a notebook and write about my life and what things i experience each and everyday but i'm sure if i was to write about myself and the things i went through and someone read it they would cry. I don't like to be open about myself, it takes me a while to open up because you can tell people everything about yourself, what you like and so on and when they're mad at you they use it against you. It's really sad when you lose the person you thought would stay for a very very very long time but the more people you lose the more you start to understand that everyone isn't who they say they are.

~

Something i hate school because when i tell something they don't understood me and but i not really good at english it hard to understand me
But i try my best and learn more than last year i like english 10 class to do work because the teacher teacher it really good toy understand i understand more in this class i happen to have a good example teacher i like to learn more and work hard this year something i love song when the teacher and nice and teach good this year i don't like the alg class because when i teacher is teach i don't like i don't understand if i don't understand when they teach i don't like school to come and the teacher is good i like to come school everyday i love to learn more i want to do hard this year
Please understand me when i say something because i not really good at speak a english because that my second legard so some question i don't really understand but i scary to ask because i scary they got angry or mad at me but anyway i like this class teach i like to learn more then more befor i really really hate english class because i dont understean and they keep ask me why u don;t know how to do i really made last year i really like this year because i understand more than last year
I learn all the time to speak english something i try to ask someone how to do and can yuo example to me i don't really understand me and one thing i don't like to talk with people because i shy to talk someone when i talk and for them i word is funny to them that why i hate school all the time my mom alway tell me never give up for school be strong and keep it up my mom is the best to keep say me that i learn i study harn and never give up to no one i do my best in class and learn more more i something i think my self i luck this year to have understand teacher and good at example
In my future i want to be fashion design or / makeup artie i nevergive up on my life if i think i do this one in my i gonna to it my family tell if you want to do something in you like don't give on it keep going keep learni favorite is fashion desigh to do when i finish the collage i ganna one the fashion store or any makeup store i gonna do it i find money by myself and give a to my family that is all my wish someone people say fashion design is hard to do

I miss my bestfriend we are friendship with on 5gread we love each other we eat together we go school together

On the high one friend is moving to dallas but something we talk about our boyfriend now we all are spread now i only have one more left beside me before we have 4 now i only have one left i miss them so much i want them back in my life i happy to have tho bestfriend in my life they make me happy and they alway are beside me when them broke up with them boyfriend we cry together and we laugh and we skip school together we got trouble in the school we have so much fun we have movement

Now in high school 12 grade some friend are marry and left in the group some are move to another state just only two more left when is rain in mind remember everything what we do what we say together sometime when is rain hard i i look at the sky and wish i have back to all my best friend like befor

~

im not who I am SORRY to be so deep

I grew up in a good place, until I got older. I was homeless, and slept on floors, ate old food cause I didn't have nothin. In & out of houses & school. I hated the way we live so I wanted to end it. Literally, I did try to attempted suicide but I fail. Cutting failed - hanging failed, just FAILED! I had reasons, I was fucking disgusting to myself. I tried again last year but I failed so I gave up. I knew it was a sign. Now, we still in a shelter, in moving in a house soon. & yes im not depressed anymore. I have a reason to be here. →

I wanna experince love, & school, and get my g.e.d. & get married & have kids.
 Im glad Im here now, & them demons are
back! NOT coming

p.s. I wanna be a theripist for childern and a mortician.

School is stressful, but I wanna sucessful.

live
live. live. live. live.
live because you have too.
Not because you want too.
Fight, that disorder.

I wish my teacher knew how much I love to do sports. My favorite sport to play is basketball of course, but I'm good at every sport if I put my mind to it. I just rather play basketball I enjoy it. When I was like eight or nine I use to play football with my big brother and his friends I enjoyed it. I wish they would make a girl football team at Northeast I would play. The feeling of playing sports is like you being real hungry and you play the sport you not even thinking about being hungry anymore. Basically what I'm saying is that when you are playing any sport it distracts your mind to the sport and then you start enjoying it once you enjoy the sport you feel yourself getting better because now you're getting the hang of everything. When I play basketball I'm not worried about nothing but the ball. Another sport that I would play but takes lots of practice is track. Everybody that seen me run know I'm fast and I know for a fact I'm fast it run through my family all my sisters played basketball and did track in highschool, and my mom just played basketball. I recommend every teen to play a sport in highschool sat all 4 because it's fun it gives you something to do after school if you not doing nothing and keeps you out of stuff you shouldn't be in. I just love the feeling of making a shot it makes me so happy. Basketball is not just a sport you get good on the second day or something it takes lots of practice sometime to learn how to dribble correctly.

I wished my teacher new that what I wanna do when I turn 12 is that I'd wanna have all my money earned from what I worked to buy myself a home to live maybe a small Apt & start being independent. Also I'd love to have at least 2 husky dogs living with me + yeah I mean all I want is a place for myself to live with husky dogs &

Another thing I wish my teacher knew is that shes one of my favs teacher because she's not like other teachers where their room is messy disorganized & Mrs. Muller room is pretty organized & has alot of posters on the wall & she's also very nice & understanding. I think Mrs. Muller should take her fav class on a field trip also maybe to a meusem where they can get to know writers since shes an english teacher. Also I'm very thanksful that day Mrs & Mr. Muller brought us pizza!

I'd like to say a little about me well my fav animal well of course know its Husky dogs! Also love trinks obvs because Im mexican

My favorite thing to do is go to the kitchen & try cooking what ever I can cook ♥ Also my favorite movie is "Ink cook of life" if you haven't watched it yet you should WATCH IT even with your husband & kids. One thing that's really important to me is all the gifts I received for my birthday or random gifts all those things are really valuable for me & I feel like I should take good care of them. One thing I hate is writing alot like right now my hand hurts ✗ Im just playing One thing I really do hate is sleeping late & waking up really early in the mornings. I am very sleepy right know & Hungry Oh my fav drink is pink drink from Starbucks. My fav color is rose gold. & I love winter ♡

I wish my teacher knew how great of a teacher she is. She explains things very well Unlike alot of the other teachers at this school she ___ ___ I pass I know this because everytime I'm not focused she always puts me on check and tells me to get back on task. She also lets me know how im doing in her class. She is probaby my favorite teacher I have alot of fun in her class, even if we do alot of work she always finds a way to make the work exciting. Sometimes I have a hard time learning and when I don't get things she always explains to me again other teachers aren't the same way. Another reason Mrs. Muller is my favorite teacher is because she rewarded us with food not many teachers do that and when they do all they give you is one piece of candy, Ms Muller let everyone get as much pizza as they wanted. I also like the fact that Ms Muller doesn't show favoritism like alot of teachers at this school do.

Acknowledgements

First and foremost, thank you, Mom & Dad, for seeing in me what I often struggle to see myself. Thank you for calling it into existence, and for steadfastly walking beside me on the very long & winding road that has been our journey together. I have been so blessed by your unconditional love and sacrifice.

Thank you, Irving, for encouraging me to chase down my dreams, and for letting me borrow some of your courage when I didn't have enough of my own. Thank you for your patience and your wisdom and the million silent ways you humbly serve and care for our family. You are the best choice I have ever made.

Thank you, Adri & Eres, for cheering me on and believing in me and being so patient with me as I've learned how to be your mama. You two are the best gifts I have ever been given. You guys have taught me that I'm so much stronger than I thought. You remind me to laugh and wonder at God's incredible goodness. Thank you for always helping me find my way back to grace.

And finally, I've saved the very best for last.

Thank you so much to my incredible students. You have absolutely changed my life. You have shared space with me with so much grace and tolerance. You have been patient with me as we have learned together how to create the best reality possible. You are some of the strongest, bravest, most creative humans I have ever met. I want you to never, ever forget that your potential in this world is limited only by your grit and your imagination. There is something inside every single one of you that this world desperately needs, and no one else can do it but you. Never believe for even a second that you aren't worthy of this calling. We need your hopes and dreams to carry us into the future. You are boundless spirit. You are fierce. You are advocates and crusaders and artists and leaders. Please, I'm begging you, show us the way.

Made in the USA
Coppell, TX
02 October 2021